The 4-4-0 Classes of the North Eastern Railway

The 4-4-0 Classes of the North Eastern Railway

K. Hoole

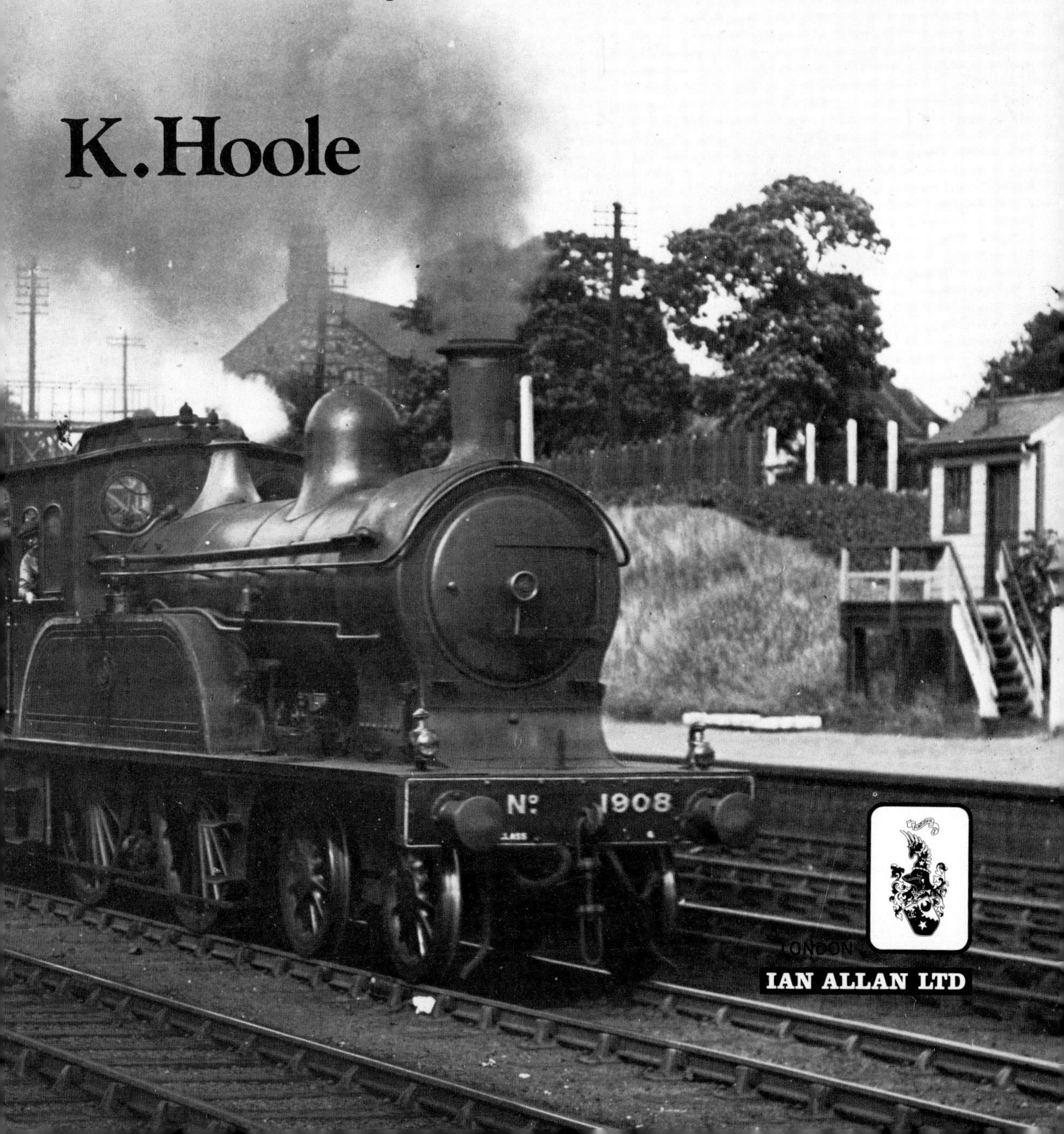

LONDON
IAN ALLAN LTD

No 1260

First published 1979

ISBN 0 7110 0921 X

Published by Ian Allan Ltd, Shepperton, Surrey; and printed in the United Kingdom by Ian Allan Printing Ltd

Contents

Introduction

The North Eastern Railway, because it did not favour the naming of locomotives, could not offer such evocative class names as the 'Dunalastairs' on the Caledonian, the 'Claud Hamiltons' on the Great Eastern, the 'Georges' and 'Precursors' on the London & North Western, or the 'Scotts' and 'Glens' of the North British. Instead, all the North Eastern could offer were the prosaic letters of the alphabet, because all the Worsdell and Raven engines were so classified, although reference to a Class M or a Class R could mean only a specific type of locomotive. However, identification of North Eastern classes was made easy when from February 1904 the class letter was painted on the front buffer-beam and was thus plainly visible to anyone interested: previously the classification had been painted in the cab.

Another way in which the North Eastern differed was that the engines under discussion were not rebuilt, or reboilered, to move them up a class, as happened, for instance, with the Great Eastern's Claud Hamilton engines, which (using the LNER classification) progressed from D14 (4ft 9in round-topped boiler) to D15 (4ft 9in Belpaire boiler) to D16 (5ft 1in Belpaire boiler) to D16/3 (Gresley round-topped boiler). The North Eastern engines remained within their own classes, although modernisation did take place with the fitting of superheaters to all Worsdell engines except one, and engines built with slide valves were rebuilt with piston valves. Other notable changes which occurred involved the abolition of the Worsdell-von Borries two-cylinder compound system, and the rebuilding of 22 2-4-0s to 4-4-0s.

The Worsdell and Raven method of engine classification was simple. Engines built from T. W. Worsdell's first design in 1886 were allocated a class letter commencing at A, progressing through the alphabet as each new class appeared, whilst engines in existence in 1886 were allocated a class number, which was actually an engine number. At first a figure 1 suffix was added to certain class letters to denote a simple engine, the basic letter, without a suffix, indicating a compound, but later the suffix figure (1, 2 or 3) came to indicate a new and improved class of engine.

With the rebuilding of the compounds to simples the letters B, C and F became blank, all the engines having been reclassified B1, C1 or F1: Class G was also blank as there were no compounds in the class. Then from 16 June 1914 it was decided to abolish the figure 1 suffix on Classes B1, C1, F1, G1, M1 and Z1, so that the three classes of 4-4-0 concerned became F, G and M. Thus, for instance, engines 1620-39 carried 'Class M1' on the front buffer-beam from 1904 to 1914, and 'Class M' from 1914 to 1932, when the LNER commenced painting the new class (D17) on the buffer-beam. Also in 1914 engine 1619, formerly Class M, was reclassified 3CC to correspond with the two 4-cylinder Smith compounds which had been Class 4CC since they were built in 1906.

When 1621 was repainted in NER livery for preservation it was given 'Class M1' on the buffer-beam — a classification which it carried for only a few weeks in its present superheated condition. It received its first superheated boiler in April 1914 and the figure 1 suffix was abolished in mid-June.

In August 1905 the North Eastern announced a scheme whereby all train engines would carry a Traffic Classification consisting of the letter T (tender engines) or K (tank engines) and a number between 1 and 10, to indicate the haulage capacity of the engine at various speeds. The classification was painted in small characters below the engine numberplate. On 12 September 1905 the works at Gateshead was instructed to apply the classification and it can be seen on contemporary photographs.

The 4-4-0 engines fell into five categories:

Class of engine	*Traffic classification*	*Tons which can be hauled on the level at speed of:* 40mph	50mph	55mph	60mph
38	T1	260	200	150	120
F F1 G1	T4	390	280	240	200
M M1	T5	420	300	260	220
Q Q1	T6	460	340	300	260
R	T8	530	410	350	300

NER Class	LNER Class	Number of engines	Compound Simple	Built	Built at	Remarks
D	D22	2	C	1886/8	Gateshead	Built as 2-4-0
F	D22	25	C	1887-91	Gateshead	
F1	D22	10	S	1887		
G1	D23	20	S	1887/8	Darlington	Built as 2-4-0
M	D19	1	C	1893	Gateshead	Built as 2-cyl compound. Rebuilt as 3-cyl compound
M1	D17/1	20	S	1892-4	Gateshead	
Q	D17/2	30	S	1896/7	Gateshead	
Q1	D18	2	S	1896	Gateshead	7ft 7¼in wheels
R	D20	60	S	1899-1907	Gateshead	
R1	D21	10	S	1908/9	Darlington	

The scheme was withdrawn from 13 June 1910 and for a time the engines were referred to solely by the tonnages quoted in the 55mph column, but this was not shown on the engine in any way. However, in December 1910 a 28 page booklet was issued giving the load for each class of engine on *all* North Eastern routes when hauling ordinary and excursion passenger trains, and also empty coaching stock trains. Separate details were issued for East Coast trains and 'all other express trains signalled E.P. on the block'.

Altogether there were 180 T. W. Worsdell and W. Worsdell 4-4-0s, built between 1886 and 1909, together with a solitary example of a Fletcher Class 901 2-4-0 rebuilt as a 4-4-0 by Wilson Worsdell in 1907 (see table above).

However, in spite of the numerous 4-4-0s built between 1887 and 1909 these were not the first of this wheel arrangement to be built for the North Eastern as Edward Fletcher ordered ten 4-4-0s from Robert Stephenson & Company for work in the Whitby area and these were delivered in 1864/5.

Over the years the Worsdell 4-4-0 engines could be seen at work all over the North Eastern system, at first on main line services and then, as they were superseded by larger engines, on services of gradually declining importance until finally, in the mid-1950s, the survivors were employed on minor services.

The last 4-4-0 was withdrawn on 20 November 1957 after 50 years work: this was 62395 (old 1260) and although attempts were made to have the engine preserved it was cut up for scrap in January 1958. However, 1621 of Class M1, built in 1893, was reprieved when it was withdrawn from service in July 1945 and it was subsequently restored to North Eastern livery and placed in the Queen Street Railway Museum at York. With the opening of the new National Railway Museum in 1975 it has been repainted and put on display there, where it provides a fine example of a late nineteenth century *English* 4-4-0, built at a time when the 4-4-0 wheel arrangement was the ultimate in British locomotive practice, although 4-4-2 and 4-6-0 engines appeared before the century was out. Not that the day of the 4-4-0 was over on the North Eastern: as already mentioned the North Eastern 4-4-0 engines continued to work until 1957, and in October 1927 the first of Gresley's three-cylinder 4-4-0s appeared from North Road Works, Darlington, in the shape of No 234 *Yorkshire.* These engines were built up to 1935, eventually totalling 76: the later engines had rotary cam operated poppet valves instead of the piston valves of the original engines. Although the majority of the Gresley engines worked in the North East a number operated in Scotland: the last in the North Eastern Region was withdrawn in January 1961, only three years after the last D20, which had appeared 20 years before the D49 design, bringing to an end 97 years of 4-4-0 operation on the North Eastern Railway and its successors.

Even so the Fletcher 'Whitby Bogie' 4-4-0s of 1864 were not the first 4-4-0s to be seen on the North Eastern as in 1860 an elaborately decorated 4-4-0 for the Copiapo & Caldera Railway in Chile, built by Kitson & Company of Leeds, was tried over the North Eastern between Leeds and Harrogate before being shipped to its destination. In the previous year, 1859, Robert Stephenson & Company of Newcastle offered to lend a 4-4-0 for trials on the Stockton & Darlington Railway: this engine was intended for the Smyrna & Aidin Railway and it had to pass over North Eastern metals to reach the Stockton & Darlington, as had the subsequent 4-4-0s ordered by the S&DR from the same locomotive builder. The final 4-4-0s for the Stockton & Darlington Section appeared in 1871(238-241) and 1874 (1265-70), after the S&DR had been absorbed by the North Eastern, but at that time the Locomotive Department was still following S&DR practice, and it was not until after the death of William

Bouch in 1876 that North Eastern influence began to make itself felt. Consequently the S&DR engines, owing nothing to North Eastern policy, are not dealt with in this work.

One difficulty in unravelling the history of North Eastern locomotives is in establishing the correct dimensions. Take, for instance, the cylinders of 1619 when built as a two-cylinder compound: *Locomotives and Railways* Vol II quotes the high pressure cylinder as 19in x 24in in the text and 20in x 24in in the table. MacLean's *Locomotives of the NER* says 19in x 26in (as does Nock, probably quoting MacLean) but the true size was 20in x 26in.

MacLean quotes the boiler pressure of the M1 engines when built as 180lb (again repeated by Nock) but in the exhaustive trials carried out by Raven and Kendal in 1893, 160lb is the figure quoted in every reference to an M1 engine, which were then only a matter of months, and even weeks, old! The company's general arrangement drawings and the early locomotive diagram books do not quote the boiler pressure, and neither does the sectional engraving published in *The Engineer* for 22 September 1893, nor the table of dimensions given in the same publication dated 27 October 1893, all obviously based on official information. Certainly the boiler pressure was later raised to 175lb (1914 diagram book) but it reverted to 160lb on superheating.

1 A General Survey

The footplate layout of all Worsdell 4-4-0s was basically the same. The driver was on the right, with the reversing screw mounted on the 'box' over the rear driving wheels. On the older classes the reversing handle was actually a wheel, but this was later changed to a bar with two handles, one of which locked the handle in the desired cut-off position. On all except Class R1 the regulator handle was of the single-bar two-handle type, moving anti-clockwise to open. The bar extended about 18in above and below the regulator rod and the ends were turned over at 90deg at top and bottom to form a convenient handle. The regulator operated in a quadrant with a stop at each end.

Lockyer double-beat regulators were subsequently fitted to many engines and these required considerably less effort to open and close: in this case there was a smaller regulator handle (about 15in above the regulator rod and with no bottom portion). There were no stops on the quadrant, which had cast on it the legend *Close the valve gently*. The Class R engines differed in that when a Lockyer regulator was fitted the regulator handle was changed to a double-armed pattern made of rectangular bar about 1¼in by ½in and this could be operated from both sides of the cab. When closed the arm on the driver's side was almost horizontal, whilst the arm on the fireman's side was at about 45deg to the horizontal. The R1 engines had the double-arm pattern from the start but, not having Lockyer regulator valves, the handle was made of 1½in dia bar with bulbous ends. This type of regulator handle was fitted to Class R engines when they lost their Lockyer regulator valves. These double-arm regulators were often referred to as 'buffalo', 'cow-horn' or 'ram's-horn' regulators.

Exceptionally the four engines rebuilt to D20 Part 2 — 592, 2020, 2102 and 62375 (ex-712) — were converted to left-hand drive, and 2020 received a completely new cab: the other three retained their North Eastern pattern cabs. In their case the regulator opened in a clockwise direction. In 1937, when modified boilers were being produced at Darlington Works, pull-out regulators were fitted to some engines (eg 2021 and 2103) but these were not a success and were removed: they tended to close with the vibration of the engine when running, but a locking device did not find favour, even though a similar type of regulator used on the Hull & Barnsley and Great Northern engines in the North Eastern Area had been held open by a wing nut.

All the cabs fitted to Worsdell engines had two openings in each side, with framed and glazed windows sliding in channels to each opening. The front windows were normally kept closed and the rear ones open, although the latter were sometimes closed if an engine was standing in a windy position. Some crews had wooden arm-rests made to fit in the grooves of the rear sliding windows: these were removed and locked in the toolbox every night!

All classes except R1 had circular front spectacle glasses in brass frames, hinged at the top. They opened inwards until the glass was horizontal, and then were held in place by a stout pin passing through a hollow circular projection at the bottom of the frame and a fitting on the cab roof. The R1 spectacles were shaped to fit the contour of the boiler and the cab roof.

The Class Q and Q1 engines were easily distinguishable by the 9½in clerestory on the roof of the cab — a design brought back from America by Wilson Worsdell. The clerestory had two horizontally pivoted vents in each side. The normal ventilation in the roof of the other classes was a hinged flap.

The chimneys of the Q and Q1 engines were embellished with a brass rim, which led to their nickname of 'Copperknobs'. Class R engines also had brass-topped chimneys but on both classes they began to disappear in the years before the Grouping, although 1258 appears to have retained a brass cap until about 1930, judging from photographs. However, this may not have been so and probably the effect was created by removing the black paint and exposing the bare metal at the appropriate spot, carried out by a crew with a pride in the appearance of their engine.

All Worsdell classes (except R1) had two-column Ramsbottom safety valves enclosed in a handsome brass trumpet. The 'tail' of the valves protruded through the cab front-plate so that it could be adjusted slightly by the crew to prevent the insistent drumming noise which occurred at times with Ramsbottom valves. The R1 engines had two pairs of Ramsbottom valves enclosed in a flattened brass trumpet, necessitated by the 5ft 6in dia boiler fitted at 8ft 7in centre line. With the continuing improvement in boilers and boiler fittings most classes received Ross 'pop' safety valves, although many of the older engines went to the scrapyard before receiving 'pop' valves. Those that did receive 'pop' valves usually had the base of the valves hidden by a neat brass cover with a flat top: on a few engines a similar but deeper cover was fitted, apparently utilising a cut-down brass trumpet. Eventually the 'pop' valves were completely bare.

With piston valve engines the NER used a vacuum-preventing and lubricating valve designed by W. M. Smith, and this was usually placed at the rear of the cylinders, although on Class R1 it was at the front. When running with steam shut off the vacuum formed in the steamchests by the pumping action of the pistons allowed a valve to rise due to atmospheric pressure. This in turn opened a steam valve allowing a small amount of steam to pass direct from the boiler into the cylinders, effectively destroying the vacuum and preventing ashes and grit in the smokebox from being drawn into the steamchest via the blastpipe. The steam also acted as a lubricator to the working surfaces thus preventing wear.

In addition the NER boilers fitted with Schmidt superheaters incorporated a steam circulating system whereby a small amount of steam was admitted to the superheater elements to prevent burning when the regulator was closed. This steam supply could be shut off by means of a small handwheel cock on the left-hand side of the smokebox — a feature which could be relied upon to indicate whether an engine was superheated or not. At one time a superheated engine on the NER could be identified by having an extended smokebox, but in LNER and BR days numerous goods and mineral engines had their superheating equipment removed, whilst retaining extended smokeboxes and piston valves. Thus the steam circulating valve (or the Gresley 'snifting' valve which replaced it) was the only sure guide externally, at least, as to whether an engine was superheated or not.

The inside frames of the 'Whitby Bogies' were ⅞in thick and 4ft 1in apart, with the outside frames 1⅛in thick. The standard Worsdell frames were 1in thick and 4ft apart, but on all 4-4-0 classes, except G and R1, the frames tapered inwards for about the front 4ft to 3ft 9½in apart. The width over the running plates was 8ft on all classes except R1, which had a width of 8ft 6in.

All boiler clothing was 3½in larger in diameter than the outside diameter of the boiler, but only on Classes 3CC and R1 was the clothing flush with the smokebox. On all the other classes the smokebox wrapper was a few inches larger in diameter than the boiler clothing, and on this type of boiler the joint was covered by a brass collar, usually kept polished in North Eastern days.

On all the Worsdell 4-4-0s (except R1) there was a small double-ended Westinghouse brake cylinder suspended between each pair of driving wheels. When the brake was applied the two pistons in the cylinder were forced outwards so that the front piston pushed a brake-block on to the rear of the leading driving wheel and pulled a block on to the rear of the rear driving wheel. The back piston pushed a block on to the front of the rear driving wheel and pulled a block on to the front of the leading driving wheel. The brake cylinders were held by a safety chain which did not appear to be very substantial. Probably it was designed to break if the cylinder did become loose and got in the way of the rapidly revolving spokes or side-rods! At very slow speeds the chain would probably be sufficient to stop a dislodged cylinder from dropping under the wheel and derailing the engine. On Class R1 braking was provided by an 18in dia push cylinder under the cab, which worked downwards and applied the brakes on the front of each driving wheel.

The Fletcher livery on the 'Whitby Bogies' included an elaborately lined-out boiler, with the boiler itself divided into four panels and the firebox into two. The lining in line with the centre of the dome bifurcated to pass back and front of the dome. Polished collars encircled the rear of the smokebox and the front of the raised firebox. The large elliptical brass numberplate was carried on the cab sides, which extended up to less than waist height, with a plain front weatherboard having two spectacles. A painted replica of the engine numberplate appeared in the centre of the tender side panels. The builder's plates were affixed on the valence above the centre of the bogie.

However, the more common photographs of these engines show them in the T. W. Worsdell livery, with claret surrounds to cab and tender, worn by the four engines which lasted until 1893.

Views of Class 38 engines in original livery and condition are very scarce and most views show them in T. W. Worsdell and Wilson Worsdell livery. It is obvious from these views in the earlier Worsdell livery that the class soon lost its McDonnell chimneys. However, two McDonnell features were retained as the engines kept their uncovered safety valves until the boilers required renewing, and also the rectangular numberplates introduced by McDonnell. These plates remained on some engines until they were withdrawn, although a few were replaced by the more familiar elliptical plates at a late stage in their existence.

In 1886 T. W. Worsdell introduced a totally new style of livery to the North Eastern, keeping to long-established green as the basic colour, but having claret borders to splashers, cabs and tanks. The first 4-4-0 design to appear in this new livery was Class F from June 1887, although No 1324, the Class D 2-4-0 later rebuilt as a 4-4-0, was turned out in the new livery in the previous year. At first the tender carried simply the letters N. E. R. in gold, shaded red, transfers, but this was soon changed to NORTH EASTERN, with a small version of the company's coat-of-arms between the two words. The engine number was carried on a large elliptical brass plate in the centre of the splashers, fixed on the left-hand side but hinged on the right splasher to give access to the almost hidden Westinghouse pump. A smaller plate denoting that the engine was a Worsdell-von Borries compound engine was fitted at the waist of the smokebox on both sides of the engine. The engine number was also carried on the front buffer-beam, with 'No.' on the left-hand side of the drawhook as viewed from in front of the engine and the actual number on the right.

The interior of the cab was wood grained in a light shade. The brass beading to the splashers, the safety valve trumpet, and the collar between the rear of the smokebox and the boiler were all highly polished.

After Wilson Worsdell had been in office for a few years he decided to modify his brother's livery, retaining the basic green but abandoning the claret borders. This livery first appeared on the Class M1 engines introduced in 1892. The elliptical numberplates on the splashers were retained, as was the NORTH EASTERN on the tender sides, but the armorial device was redesigned.

This basic livery using Saxony green was retained for the remainder of the North Eastern's existence, the only alteration being the introduction of a larger and more elaborate armorial device introduced on the tender from c1900.

It was NER practice to keep engine and tender regularly paired, and the engine number was depicted in gold transfers on the flare at the top of the back panel on the tender. The R1 engines carried the small version of the armorial device in the centre of the leading splashers, and with having separate splashers, the numberplate was placed in the centre of the rear splasher. In all cases smokeboxes and smokebox doors were black. From 1905 to 1910 a loading classification was carried below the engine numberplate as described in the Introduction: this consisted of the letter T followed by a number between 1 and 10. The engine classification appeared in the cab from 1901 but was transferred to the front buffer-beam, below the number, in 1904.

In his *Locomotive & Train Working in the Nineteenth Century* E. L. Ahrons describes how North Eastern crews at one time adorned their engines with pictures of lightly clad females, and how this was looked upon disapprovingly. Probably because of this incident, decorations on North Eastern engines were still rare in Worsdell and Raven days, but some engines did appear with small designs on the smokebox where the paint had been scraped away to show the design in bare metal. Engines of classes F, M1, Q, R and R1 were all noted with one of these small embellishments.

From 1923 the North Eastern 4-4-0s continued to appear in a green livery, but of a darker shade as standardised by the LNER. The large brass number-plates were removed and the engine number applied on tender sides by means of 12in transfers, above which was L. & N. E. R., L & N E R, or L N E R in 7½in transfers.

The LNER fitted all engines with a small cast elliptical building plate based on the design introduced in 1917 by the NER on goods engines as a wartime economy measure. The number continued to appear on the front bufferbeam but there was now no need for the engine number to appear on the back of the tender. In 1928 it was decided that all the ex-North Eastern 4-4-0s should be included in the classes to be painted black, lined red, as a further economy measure, but some engines, such as D19 No 1619, did not receive the new livery and went to the scrapheap still in the LNER green.

Until Gateshead Works closed in 1932 engines repainted there had their cab interiors finished in green, whereas Darlington painted their's red.

In 1929 a new directive led to the number being put on the engine itself, leaving only L N E R on the tender. This new scheme meant that the number disappeared off the tender completely and therefore new numberplates had to be cast so that the tender could be identified when separated from the engine, and these plates were affixed in the centre of the rear panel of the tender. Yet further economy studies showed that a tender normally needed less time for repairs than the engine, and on visits to the works the tender was often standing idle awaiting the completion of repairs to the engine. Thus in 1938, to allow tenders to be changed around more easily, all North Eastern Area tenders were allocated a number from 7001 upwards, in a separate series of numbers which bore no connection with the engine number.

About 1890 the Class F engines carried details of the engine and crew on the two toolboxes across the front of the tender. On one, in letters about 3in high was, for instance:

COMPOUND PASSENGER
ENGINE No 117

and on the other:

ROBERT NICHOLSON DRIVER
GATESHEAD

From about 1896 to 1900 the layout on the front

buffer-beam was changed and the engine number was placed above the drawhook.

About 1913 the 3-cylinder compound No 1619 was noted with CLASS M1 on the front buffer-beam, whereas at that time it was Class M.

The North Eastern class continued to be painted on the front buffer-beam of all the 4-4-0s until 1932 when, nine years after the Grouping, it was replaced by the LNER class.

In North Eastern days engines did not usually carry any indication of their home shed, although some depots did paint the shed name on the engine headlamps. In early LNER days the shed was painted in the cab in an abbreviated form, but this was superseded by a narrow enamelled plate in the 1930s. However, these plates did not stand up to the corrosive fumes in the cab and some sheds bolted them to the front buffer-beam, whilst others stencilled an abbreviated name in the same place. Finally many of the D20 engines carried the standard shed-plate on the smokebox door.

The North Eastern Railway was not very explicit in specifying lines over which certain classes of locomotive could, or could not, work, and the 1922 WTT Appendix listed only two lines over which all 4-4-0s were prohibited, namely Selby-Cawood and Castleton-Grosmont.

Line	*Classes Prohibited*	*Classes Allowed*
Axholme Joint	M, Q, Q1, R, R1, 3CC	F and G
Barnard Castle-Kirkby Stephen	F, M, Q, Q1, R, R1, 3CC	G
Castleton-Grosmont	F, G, M, Q, Q1, R, R1, 3CC	Nil
Otley-Ilkley	M, Q, Q1, R, R1, 3CC	F and G
Selby-Cawood	F, G, M, Q, Q1, R, R1, 3CC	Nil
Wear Valley Junction-Wearhead	F, M, Q, Q1, R, R1, 3CC	G
Whitby-Pickering	3CC	F, G, M, Q, Q1, R, R1

The LNER Appendix of 1931 used LNER classes but the effect was still the same except that Castleton-Grosmont and the Wear Valley lines were unrestricted, and the Whitby-Pickering section restriction had disappeared because engine No 1619 had been withdrawn.

Immediately prior to World War II the position was:

Line	*Classes Prohibited*	*Classes Allowed*
Barnard Castle-Kirkby Stephen	D17/1, D17/2, D20, D21	Nil
Barnard Castle-Middleton in Teesdale Otley-Ilkley	D21	D17/1, D17/2, D20
Bradford-Otley Bradford-Ilkley	D21	D17/1, D17/2, D20

In 1914 F1 No 1 was renumbered 356 when it was decided to include the electric and steam locomotives in one list. Since the building of the Quayside electric locomotive No 1 in 1904 there had been two engines carrying No 1 in service on the NER — one steam and one electric!

When in 1943 the LNER decided to renumber all its locomotives new numbers were allocated to 73 former NER 4-4-0s, but by the time the scheme was implemented in 1946 only 56 remained to be renumbered, comprising two D17/2 and 54 D20s. Of the D20s renumbered into the 23xx series between 2340 and 2397 only 43 survived long enough to receive the figure six prefix indicating BR ownership. Details of these renumberings are given in the tables of individual classes.

In 1923, as an interim measure, some engines had a letter D suffix added to their numbers to indicate that they were North Eastern Area stock; the suffix indicated Darlington, no allowance being made for the fact that many ex-NER 4-4-0s were maintained at Gateshead Works. Similarly, in 1948 some engines had a letter E prefix added to their numbers to indicate that they were Eastern and North Eastern Region stock. Details of these suffixes are not included in the tables.

To me the reason for the movement of a locomotive from one shed to another provides a fascinating study. Unfortunately it is usually impossible to appreciate the reasons for such transfers without 'inside information' but a study of the North Eastern Area transfers in the 1920s and 1930s elicits the following:

214 D23 Malton to Hull in exchange for G5 1703 when a tank engine was required at Malton because the turntable there was under repair.

Triangular moves were fairly common; for instance in May 1925 D17/1 No 1637 was displaced from Tweedmouth and transferred to Selby: this in turn displaced D22 No 1532 from Selby to Hull to release D23 No 258 to move to Tweedmouth to work on the Border branches.

Five months later the National Union of Railwaymen complained about a Westinghouse-fitted engine being provided to assist the vacuum-braked 4.17pm Newcastle to Liverpool from Ripon to Leeds. Consequently D22 No 1541 (vacuum and Westinghouse-fitted) was transferred from Scarborough to Starbeck, displacing D23 No 1120 from Starbeck to Hull, which in turn displaced D22 No 42 (Westinghouse only) from Hull to Scarborough, thus replacing No 1541. Within a matter of days No 1541 required repairs and No 1537 of the same class (also dual-fitted) had to be borrowed from Selby.

In the summer months it was the practice to transfer engines from the Northern Division to the Southern Division to help out with the holiday traffic. Thus in May 1925 D17/1 No 1621 went from Tweedmouth to Selby, followed in July 1925 by D20 No 723 from Tweedmouth to Scarborough, where it was joined by D17/2 No 1928 from Gateshead and No 1930 from West Hartlepool. No 1928 went home in the following month but No 723 and No 1930 did not return north until October; No 1621 actually remained at Selby until January 1926.

Engines were sometimes moved for working specific trains, such as D21 No 1241 from York to Starbeck on 19 September 1925 in readiness for working the 'West Riding Pullman' to Leeds when it commenced to run two days later. In April 1925 D21 No 1246 was transferred from York to Hull to work the 2.50pm to Sheffield and two months later it was joined by No 1245 of the same class, also from York; No 1240 from Leeds followed in January 1926.

Class D20 No 725 was moved from Leeds to Scarborough in January 1926 for use on the 8.25am Scarborough-Hull express, although Scarborough shed already had three D20s — No 708, No 724 and No 2013. In July 1927 D17/2 No 1929 was sent from Gateshead to Saltburn to work a regular express passenger train to York, but a few weeks later it failed and No 1922 had to be borrowed from West Hartlepool. Two years later Saltburn acquired D22 No 684 from Selby to work the 9.14am to Leeds but it was returned to Selby a fortnight later as 'not strong enough'! No replacement engine is recorded.

The bringing into service of new engines usually displaced older engines one step further down the ladder, those at the bottom going for scrap. If an engine was withdrawn by the Works a replacement of a similar type had to be found to work the services, such as when D23 No 23 was withdrawn from Waskerley in July 1929 and it had to be replaced by No 678 of the same class from Darlington. Sometimes when a class was being steadily withdrawn an engine of a larger type had to be provided, as when D22 No 779 was withdrawn from Scarborough in February 1930 and the replacement was D20 No 712 from York.

When D17/1 No 1636 was required at Northallerton in May 1930 for working a Hawes to York milk train, D20 No 1672 was sent from York to Darlington to replace it, and York received C6 No 701 from Gateshead as a replacement for No 1672.

Throughout the 1930s the North Eastern Area carried out a rationalisation programme under which an attempt was made to reduce the variety of engines at a shed, and to concentrate engines of one class at as few sheds as possible. For instance in April 1931, D21 Nos 1239/40/5/6 went from Hull to Leeds to have 'all class D21 at one shed' — but No 1241 and No 1242 remained at Starbeck! In exchange Hull received D20s Nos 1026 and 2109 from Leeds, and two K3 2-6-0s from Dairycoates.

An unusual move took place in November 1931 when D20 No 2027 of York was exchanged for No 1207 of Heaton: this was because Heaton required an engine with steam heater connections at both ends for a tender-first working, and whereas No 2027 was so fitted No 1207 had heater connections at the rear end only.

In February 1934 D20 No 2101, fitted with a patent blastpipe (of which details are not known), was to be tried out in the Hull area and consequently it was transferred from York in exchange for No 2017.

New D49 engines at Scarborough caused an upheaval in 1934, displacing D20s Nos 725 and 1147 to Selby and 712 to Starbeck, and D17/2 Nos 1906 and 1907 to West Hartlepool. No 1147 returned to Scarborough later in the year in exchange for D17/2 No 1902 as Scarborough needed a more powerful engine, and 1902 was considered more suitable for use at Selby.

New D49s to Gateshead displaced D20s Nos 1184 to Stockton, 1209, 1223, 1235 and 2030 to West Hartlepool, and 1236, 2104 and 2105 to Starbeck, all on 15 April 1935. The four engines sent to West Hartlepool displaced D17/2 Nos 1879 and 1906 to Alnmouth, and 1871 and 1873 to Hull.

It was not often that a 4-4-0 was transferred for a freight working, but on 11 June 1936 D20 No 476 was moved from Heaton to Haverton Hill to work the 1.10pm SX Haverton Hill South to York (Dringhouses) conveying Drikold dry ice from the ICI works at Billingham: this working ceased in October the same year and No 476 moved across the Tees to Middlesbrough shed.

2 Development and Special Fittings

Walter Muckersie* Smith joined the North Eastern in 1883 after a wide experience of locomotives with Neilson & Company, the Edinburgh & Glasgow Railway, the Great Eastern, and the Imperial Government Railways of Japan. His introduction to NER locomotives was during the reign of Alexander McDonnell and nothing is known of their relationship; however, Smith was already installed at Gateshead when T. W. Worsdell arrived to take charge in 1885, and with both having worked on the Great Eastern they appear to have been complementary in that Smith was allowed to try out some of his ideas on Worsdell's engines. As is well known this relationship continued after T. W. Worsdell had been succeeded by his brother Wilson in 1890, culminating in the appearance of the two Smith four-cylinder compound Atlantics in 1906.

In addition to his compounding ideas, Smith was also particularly interested in piston valves and in 1888 Class D 2-4-0 No 340 was turned out fitted with three piston valves, one 7in dia for the high-pressure cylinder, and two 5½in dia for the low-pressure cylinder. These were inside admission valves but they were removed when the engine was rebuilt to an F1 4-4-0 in 1896. Next came the fitting of piston valves to Class C1 0-6-0 No 107 in 1891, followed by the fitting to the last of the Class M1 engines (1639) in 1894. The latter were of the segmental type with outside admission; three segments of the head (normally held in place by the steam pressure) could move inwards to allow the escape of any water trapped in the cylinder. This type of valve was also fitted to the Class J 'singles' in 1895/6 when they were rebuilt from Worsdell-von Borries compounds to simples. However, the first complete class to be fitted with Smith piston valves from the outset was the Class R 4-4-0, introduced in 1899, and altogether 60 engines were built. From that time piston valves were used in all new North Eastern passenger engines, including the last 4-4-0s built for the Company, the large R1 engines of 1908. Both the R and R1 engines were saturated to begin with but they were fitted with superheated boilers later; on the other Worsdell 4-4-0s — Classes F, G, M, Q, and Q1 — piston valves were provided when a superheated boiler was fitted.

*Spelling used in obituary notice in *Proc Inst Mech Engs* 1906.

Piston Valves

Class	*Diameter of valves*	*Remarks*
Classes built with piston valves		
D	1 HP 7in 2 LP 5½in	Engine 340 only
M1	7½in	Engine 1639 only
R	8¾in	60 engines
R1	10in	10 engines
Classes rebuilt with piston valves		
3CC	1 HP 8in	Engine 1619
F1	7½in	45 engines
G1	7½in	20 engines
M1	8¾in	20 engines
Q	8¾in	30 engines
Q1	8¾in	2 engines
Classes rebuilt with larger piston valves		
D20/2	10in	Engines 592, 2020, 2101 and 62375 (ex 712)

Water Tubes

Mr W. M. Smith was also allowed to experiment with water tubes in the fireboxes of two 4-4-0 engines, but details are difficult to locate. First to be fitted was Q No 1929 when built at Gateshead in November 1897 and, judging from a drawing in *Engineering* in January 1902, it had 12 cross-firebox water tubes 1½in external diameter. These ran from the top corner of the firebox, then horizontally across the box approximately 9in below the crown, to the opposite side of the box about 15in down from the top. The water tubes ran alternately from the left top corner to the right side, and from the right top corner to the left side, with the horizontal portion of the tubes in line about 4in apart along the firebox. According to figures quoted in the article, No 1929 used 5.4lb of coal per mile less than similar engines without water tubes employed on the same duties, giving a total saving over six months and 27,598 miles of 66½ tons of coal!

When 1619 was rebuilt as a three-cylinder compound in 1898 it was also fitted with water tubes, in this case 17, giving a heating surface of:

Firebox	118.5sq ft
Tubes	1,171.0sq ft
Water tubes	39.0sq ft
Total	1,328.5sq ft

No signs of the water tubes could be seen from outside the engine and it seems that it was impossible to get at them for descaling without removing them one by one from inside the firebox.

Two years later a new firebox was fitted, this time having three sets of seven water tubes crossing the firebox in a brief spiral. Each group of tubes could be examined externally and for this purpose three covers were provided on each side of the firebox, each covered by a 'blister' to maintain the green livery of the engine. The 'blisters' were not the same on each side of the engine; on the right-hand side there were two in line, with the third placed centrally but at a lower level. On the left-hand side the two in line were in the lower position, with the third placed centrally but at a higher level.

O O
O
Right

O
O O
Left

A slight reduction in heating surface resulted:

Firebox		118.60sq ft
Tubes		1,171.28sq ft
Water tubes		34.12sq ft
	Total	1,324.00sq ft

No details of the performance of the water tubes has been located, either in NER records or in published accounts, but 1619 received a new firebox in 1906 and it is assumed that this was when the engine lost its water tubes. A new boiler was fitted in September 1913 and this lasted for the remainder of the engine's life.

Fireboxes

The fireboxes fitted to the D, F/F1, G1, and M/M1 4-4-0s were all placed between the axles, with the grate sloping down towards the front, the rear end of the grate being some 2ft below the bottom of the firehole. On 1619 in its rebuilt form a firebox 8ft long was fitted, compared with the 6ft 9in of the original, giving a grate area of 23sq ft compared with the 19.5sq ft of the original. This necessitated the rear end of the firebox being placed above the rear axle and the grate still sloped down towards the front. Consequently the back end of the firegrate was on a level with the cab floor, and only by raising the firehole was it possible to obtain about 15in depth between the bottom of the firehole and the grate.

The Class R engines reverted to a firebox between the axles, but with a level grate, whereas the R1 engines had a long grate similar to that on 1619, with the back end above the rear axle. However, on this final NER 4-4-0 design the rear half of the grate was level and only the front half sloped downwards. Again the back end of the grate was level with the cab floor, necessitating a high firehole. The firebox on Class R1 was 9ft long, with a grate area of 27sq ft.

Special Fittings

In May 1902 Gateshead Works was instructed to equip three Class R engines for oil fuel, but two months later only 2028 was specified. So far no details have been located although it is known that the system used was Holden's.

The North Eastern dynamometer car was ready for use in March 1906 and in that month 2109 worked preliminary runs to allow the staff to become accustomed to the apparatus. In the following July 4-4-0s 2021, 2027 and 2107 were tried out using the dynamometer car on express goods trains with 25% of the wagons braked, and in September 2021 was used on vacuum brake trials.

A number of tests with new equipment took place in 1907. In May 1907 a drawing was prepared for the fitting of a turbo-dynamo on a Class R and the *Dynamometer Car Log Book* shows that 713 ran 'electric light trials' on 28 January 1907. Again no details appear to have survived. In April and July 1907 No 2027 was testing valve settings and at the end of the year it was on consumption tests. Also in December 1907 Nos 1042 and 2024 were on brake tests.

On 16 January 1908 No 2018 was used to test a Murphy depth gauge, which indicated electrically in the dynamometer car the depth of water in the tender. Water consumption tests with 1051, 1209 and 2027 followed in February 1908 and in April 1908 exhaustive tests of the Maximus brake commenced, lasting intermittently until August 1909. The Maximus brake actually used the normal Westinghouse brake but on each bogie the brake rigging was so arranged that the pressure of the brake blocks on the wheels was automatically reduced as the speed decreased, securing constant retardation.

On 20 May 1908 No 1210 ran a test run with a spark arrester, and on 17 June it was again tried, but this time with the spark arrester removed. Nos 1223 and 1260 were also tried with spark arresters later the same year. When 1235 was built in 1907 it was modified by having an extended smokebox fitted. It is possible that this was in connection with some form of superheater, but the first mention of such equipment on this engine is not until 13 March 1908 when it ran superheater trials with the dynamometer car. Further trials commenced on 20 April 1909, when 1235 was recorded as having 'Sisterson superheater (large) in' and a second series from 20 May 1909 with 'Sisterson superheater (large) out'. A few months later 1078 was tried with a Robinson superheater. However, the North Eastern eventually decided on the Schmidt pattern and this type was first fitted into 1235 in November 1913 and 1078 in June 1914.

In July 1907 Wilson Worsdell (together with W. R. Preston) patented a design of variable blastpipe and this was used on numerous engines, including the Class R 4-4-0s. In January 1909 Mr Worsdell reported to the Locomotive & Stores Committee that he had made arrangements with Messrs Stone & Company for them to handle the promotion of the variable blastpipe 'on the understanding that the NER shall, in perpetuity, have the right of free use'.

In 1894 Vincent Raven (who was appointed Chief Mechanical Engineer of the NER in 1910) was allowed to instal a type of fog signalling apparatus on certain engines, with the necessary ground equipment at Merrybent Junction and Shildon Tunnel. The apparatus was patented in 1895 and in 1900 instructions were given that all Class R engines should be so fitted.

The apparatus consisted of a striker suspended below the engine, which struck a raised arm when passing a distant signal at 'caution'. At the same time the Westinghouse brakes were partially applied and a compressed air whistle operated in the cab. No indication was given if the distant signal was at 'clear', and the apparatus was not fitted at stop signals. This system remained in use until October 1933 when the installation of colour-light signals on the main line made much of the equipment redundant.

In 1907 an electrical form of the apparatus was installed on the main line between Durham and Bensham and certain Class R engines were fitted with an indicator in the cab which repeated the indication of the semaphore signals on the lineside. Engines fitted with this type of gear can be identified in photographs by a rotary switch mounted on an arm extending out from the bogie frame on each side of the engine. When rotated by lineside ramps the rotary switch caused a bell warning signal to be given in the cab, informing the driver that he was approaching a location where an indication would be given which corresponded with that given by the distant signal. With an improved version of this equipment the indication of stop signals could be repeated in the cab, even to showing which route was signalled at a diverging junction. However, because of its complexity the electrical system did not have a very long life and the more simple mechanical system outlasted if by many years.

In April 1931 No 476 was fitted with an audible fog signalling apparatus marketed by Messrs Gresham & Craven. As with the Raven system this was designed to blow a whistle in the cab and partially apply the vacuum brakes at a distant signal, but after extensive tests, again at Merrybent Junction, the system was not taken up by the LNER.

In 1909 drawings were prepared for fitting a Maclean's Draught Inducer to two engines, a Q and a G1, but it has been possible to trace only the fitting of this apparatus to G1 No 557, a photograph of which turned up many years ago in Stephenson & Hawthorn's files in Newcastle! This shows a cylindrical metal jacket fitted around the engine chimney, with what appears to be an adjustable ventilator fitted in a forward-facing position at the base of the jacket. A control wire passed back to the cab via various pulleys so that the ventilator could be opened or closed by the driver to vary the draught up the jacket and around the chimney top. At the time of the experiment 557 was stationed at Hull and the photograph mentioned above shows it standing in Paragon station in Hull.

Even the whistle and whistle gear varied over the years. Take the Class R engines: at the time they were built the NER standard was a U-shaped pipe mounted vertically on top of the firebox in the cab and projecting through the cab roof. Each pipe was surmounted by a bell type whistle but they were not the same size, as one was the warning whistle and the other was the brake whistle; the latter was used when braking was required from the guard (or guards) manning the train. This was a relic of the days of non-automatic brakes on passenger trains, but still necessary when working unfitted freights over hilly lines.

In the final days of the NER the U-shaped pipe and whistles were transferred outside the cab, usually when the boiler was fitted with Ross 'pop' safety valves in place of the original Ramsbottom pattern. Changes in the type of whistle also began to take place as organ pipe whistles (previously used only on shunting engines) were substituted for the bell type.

In 1935 the LNER started fitting a redesigned type of whistle gear to former North Eastern engines and on the D20s this resulted in a single whistle, mounted vertically at the end of a horizontal pipe projecting through the front plate of the cab. However, these were prone to 'necking' and in 1937 the single bell whistle was mounted on the firebox top between the cab and the safety valves, but even this design varied. At first it was just a plain pipe with the whistle mounted at the top, but later a cock was incorporated into the base of the whistle so that steam could be shut off from the whistle if so required.

During World War II many of the engines retaining the U-shaped pipe and two whistles had the whistle on the fireman's side removed and that end of the pipe blanked off. Finally, a single whistle projecting throught the cab roof was used.

3 Class 492 – Fletcher 4-4-0 Introduced 1864

In 1845, just prior to the opening of the York to Scarborough line and the branch from Rillington to Pickering, the York and North Midland Railway purchased the little horse-worked Whitby & Pickering Railway. This had been opened throughout on 26 May 1836 as the first step in providing an outlet from Whitby to the south. Because of the light construction of the Whitby & Pickering steps were immediately taken to upgrade the line so that it could take steam locomotives, and in the relevant Act of 30 June 1845 extensive deviations were authorised. The use of steam locomotives was also authorised, but even so locomotives from the Pickering end could work only as far as the top of the Goathland rope-worked incline, and Whitby engines only as far as the foot of the same incline: the first locomotive to reach Whitby arrived on 4 June 1847.

A major work during the improvements was the building of a larger tunnel at Grosmont, alongside the original tunnel, but even after the extensive alterations to the line there were still many sharp curves and the locomotives were restricted to 0-4-0 tender engines with four-wheel tenders built in the 1840s. In the late 1850s the firm of Robert Stephenson & Company of Newcastle was developing the 4-4-0 engine and one intended for the Smyrna & Aidin Railway was tried out on various railways, notably the Stockton & Darlington, which subsequently ordered similar engines for use on the line over Stainmore Summit from Darlington to Barnard Castle, Kirkby Stephen and Tebay. Obviously the Locomotive Superintendent of the North Eastern, Edward Fletcher, took note of

Below: Class 492. One of the 'Whitby Bogies' in original condition. / *Author's collection*

these developments and he ordered ten 4-4-0 engines for use on the Malton, Pickering and Whitby line, although it must be stressed that these engines bore little resemblance to the Smyrna & Aidin and Stockton & Darlington engines. However, they did provide a means of getting a larger engine whilst retaining a minimum fixed wheelbase.

These engines, NER 492-501 (Stephenson 1581-90), were delivered between September 1864 and June 1865, having 5ft 0¼in driving wheels and 16in x 22in inside cylinders. The coupled wheelbase was 7ft 8in and the bogie wheelbase 4ft 0in, with bogie wheels 3ft 0⅜in diameter. The distance between the rear bogie wheels and the leading driving wheels was 5ft 3in, giving a total engine wheelbase of 16ft 11in. The boiler was 10ft 6in long and 4ft 0in diameter.

The bogie was set well back so that the centre line was actually 6in behind the rear edge of the smokebox. The two cylinders under the smokebox had their slide valves between them. Outside frames were fitted to the driving wheels. Screw reverse with a horizontal thread was fitted on the right-hand side of the footplate, and at first the crew's only protection was a plain weatherboard containing two 16in dia spectacles. The boiler was surmounted by a large bell-mouthed dome with two Salter safety valves, and a typical Fletcher stovepipe chimney.

Water gauges were not fitted and the level of the water in the boiler was determined by two test cocks, one 2in above the firebox crown, and the other 4in above that. Other cab fittings were simply the regulator, a pressure gauge, two whistles, injector control on the left-hand side, and crosshead pump control on the right-hand side.

The weight on the bogie was 11tons 8cwt, and on the driving wheels 12tons 17cwt and 7tons 16cwt. The bogie wheels had compensated springing with underhung springs, later changed to inverted outside springs bearing on the tops of the axleboxes.

The maker's plates were affixed to the running plate valence above the bogie, but it became North Eastern policy not to display such plates and they were removed, although the resulting difference in the thickness of the paint could be seen until the engines were scrapped. The engines originally carried a typical North Eastern elliptical brass numberplate on the cab side sheets, with a painted replica on the tender, although towards the end of their careers they had N. E. R. on the tender.

The four engines surviving until 1893 as 1807-1810 had cabs fitted at some time, as the well-known Locomotive Publishing Company's photograph by B. Mashiter of Whitby shows. However, it should be noted that there are two views in existence, taken at the same time, which differ only in the way the steam from the safety valves is blowing in the wind!

It seems probable that these ten engines were ordered with three developments in view:

1 The impending completion of the Goathland diversion to avoid the rope-worked incline, thus allowing through locomotive workings between Whitby and Malton. The deviation line was opened on 1 July 1865.

Below: Class 492. No 500 at Malton; modified with inverted springs to bogie. Note small sandbox. This engine was withdrawn in September 1894. / *LPC*

2 The impending completion of a curve at Rillington to allow through running from Whitby to Scarborough, also opened on 1 July 1865. This line was built to stifle competition from an independent company planning a direct route from Whitby to Scarborough.

3 The impending completion of the line between Grosmont and Castleton, thus allowing through workings between Whitby and Stockton. This section had originally been authorised by the York & North Midland Act of 1846, but it was allowed to lapse and the line was built under a North Eastern Act of 1861. It was opened on 2 October 1865.

Although the Goathland Deviation line and the Grosmont-Castleton section filled obvious needs the Scarborough service via the Rillington curve was not a great success and the average number of passengers per day amounted to only 31, or eight per train: the receipts per day came to £5 1s 9½d (£5 9p) or £1 5s 5½d (£1 27p) per train. Not surprisingly the service was withdrawn from 1 October 1866 — although the line against which it was intended to compete did not materialise until 1885 in the form of the Scarborough & Whitby Railway. Until then passengers between the two coastal towns changed at Rillington, or more often at Malton.

Thus although the ten 4-4-0 engines are often considered as working solely between Whitby and Malton there were plenty of engines to work also from Whitby to Stockton. It is also possible that after the opening of the Scarborough & Whitby Railway in 1885 the survivors worked over that line but no proof of this has so far been located.

Between Whitby and Malton the trains were allowed 90 to 100min for the 35¼ miles; between Whitby and Stockton 125min for the 43¾ miles with trains on both lines stopping at all stations. The Whitby-Scarborough expresses, stopping only at Pickering, were allowed 90min for the 47 miles.

Three engines were withdrawn from service in 1883/4 under their original numbers, 497, 498 and 500, and three more went for scrap in 1888 under duplicate numbers 1710 (493), 1712 (494) and 1713 (499). The remaining engines were reboilered as they were 'shopped' between 1882 and 1886, but all four, Nos 1807 (492), 1808 (495), 1809 (496) and 1810 (501) disappeared in the last three months of 1893, with an average total mileage of 726,053 per engine. Nos 1807 and 1809 were withdrawn from Whitby shed, 1810 from Malton, and surprisingly 1808 from Tweedmouth, where it presumably finished its days on branch line services.

The engines withdrawn in 1883/4 and 1888 retained their original iron boilers until the end; of the reboilered engines 492, 495 and 501 received

Below: Class 492. A fine view of 1809 (originally 496) at Whitby shed c1893. The livery is the T. W. Worsdell version with claret borders to cab, sandboxes, tender etc. Builder's plate removed. Inadequate sandboxes replaced by much larger version. Square cab. An almost identical photograph is in existence, obviously taken at the same time, the only difference between the two being that the steam from the safety valves on the dome is blowing in the opposite direction. / *LPC*

replacement iron boilers, but 496 received a steel boiler.

Nos 1710, 1712 and 1713 were cut up at Darlington in 1888 but the frames of two, 1712 and 1713, were sent to Gateshead to be converted to snowploughs, although it has proved impossible to identify any such ploughs. No 1808 was cut up at Percy Main on 5 October 1893.

Above: Class 492. No 1810 (ex-501), also in T. W. Worsdell livery, in the yard at Darlington Works, probably in the 1890s. A Worsdell pattern chimney has replaced the Fletcher stovepipe; a rounded cab has been fitted, and coal rails have been added to the tender. The large building in the background is the granary owned by Pease & Partners, colliery and quarry owners. / *LPC*

Class 492 Built by Robert Stephenson & Co

Engine		*Built*	*Renumbered*		*Reboilered*		*Cut up/ Replaced/ Withdrawn*	*Total Engine Mileage*	*Notes*
492	RS 1581	9/64	1807	1-7-89	Iron	11/85	12/93	754,105	1 and 4
493	RS 1582	9/64	1710	1-87	—	—	2/88	—	
494	RS 1583	11/64	1712	1-87	—	—	4/88	—	
495	RS 1584	3/65	1808	1-7-89	Iron	4/86	10/93	624,672	2 and 5
496	RS 1585	3/65	1809	1-7-89	Steel	5/83	11/93	775,737	1 and 6
497	RS 1586	3/65	——		—	—	9/83	—	
498	RS 1587	4/65	——		—	—	3/84	—	
499	RS 1588	4/65	1713	1-87	—	—	3/88	—	
500	RS 1589	4/65	——		—	—	9/84	—	
501	RS 1590	5/65	1810	1-7-89	Iron	7/82	11/93	749,699	3 and 7

Notes

1 Withdrawn from Whitby shed
2 Withdrawn from Tweedmouth shed
3 Withdrawn from Malton shed
4 Mileage of original boiler 562,036. Mileage of new boiler 192,069
5 Mileage of original boiler 507,756. Mileage of new boiler 116,916
6 Mileage of original boiler 543,794. Mileage of new boiler 231,943
7 Mileage of original boiler 511,476. Mileage of new boiler 238,223

4 Class 38 – McDonnell 4-4-0 Introduced 1884

In July 1882 Alexander McDonnell from the Great Southern & Western Railway (of Ireland) was appointed Locomotive Superintendent of the North Eastern to succeed Edward Fletcher from 1 November 1882, starting at a salary of £1,600 per annum, plus a free house. His first design for the North Eastern was a 0-6-0 tender engine, which became Class 59, and 44 of these were built between September 1883 and September 1885, 32 at the Company's own works at Darlington, and 12 by Robert Stephenson & Company at Newcastle. The last of these six-coupled engines was withdrawn in December 1930.

Next came a design of 4-4-0, later known as Class 38, of which 16 were built at Gateshead Works between February and December 1884; in addition 12 were built by R. & W. Hawthorn of Newcastle between October 1884 and April 1885. The Gateshead batch took vacant numbers between 38 and 1331, whereas the Hawthorn engines were numbered consecutively from 1492 to 1503; however, the two batches could also be distinguished by the shape of the running plate and splashers over the coupled wheels. On the Hawthorn engines the running plate did not rise as high as on the Gateshead version and consequently the curves at front and rear were flatter, and the splashers over the leading driving wheels were deeper, as were the cab side sheets over the rear coupled wheels.

These 4-4-0s were very similar in appearance to the engines McDonnell had produced at Inchicore between 1877 and 1880; in fact in an official North

Below: Class 38. Photographs of McDonnell engines in original condition are scarce; this view shows 186. / *L. Ward collection*

Eastern publication of 1893 a photograph of GS&W No 53 was reproduced and captioned as being a McDonnell 4-4-0 for the North Eastern, whereas it was actually to a later design by his successor at Inchicore, J. F. Aspinall! The Irish engines were built to the 5ft 3in gauge, but even so they were smaller than those for the North Eastern.

		GS&W	NER
Cylinders		16in x 20in	17in x 24in
Driving wheels		5ft 8½in	6ft 8¼in
Bogie wheels		3ft 0in	3ft 1¼in
Engine wheelbase		18ft 8¾in	20ft 10½in
Boiler length		9ft 4in	10ft 3in
Boiler diameter		3ft 9¾in	4ft 3in
Heating surface:	firebox	83.8sq ft	104.25sq ft
	tubes	770.0sq ft	926.00sq ft
	Total	853.8sq ft	1,030.25sq ft
Grate area		16.0sq ft	16.80sq ft
Tubes 1¾in dia		175	193
Boiler pressure		150lb/in^2	140lb/in^2

Between August 1895 and August 1900 all 28 North Eastern engines were fitted with a Worsdell pattern boiler and apart from the different dimensions (see later) the new boilers could be distinguished by having clack valves on each side and Ramsbottom safety valves covered by a polished brass trumpet. The McDonnell boiler had a mudhole/manhole on the bottom of the front ring but this was not perpetuated on the Worsdell boilers.

The story has been told and retold of how the North Eastern footplate crews disliked the McDonnell engines, largely because of the abolition of exhaust cocks (whereby exhaust steam could be allowed to escape without passing through the blastpipe), the introduction of left-hand drive after almost 60 years of right-hand drive; and the use of a chimney which tapered from the bottom, instead of from the top as on Fletcher chimneys, which were a severe stovepipe pattern anyway. McDonnell also changed the shape of the engine numberplates from elliptical to rectangular but the men do not seem to have claimed that this fact also altered the efficiency of the engine!

There was also some difficulty over the wheelbase of 41ft 6¼in which would not allow the engines to be turned on a 42ft 0in turntable. Although the engines would just sit on a turntable of that size there had to be some latitude for the difference in weight between engine and tender because usually, when balanced, the engine wheelbase was not symmetrical about the centre pivot of the turntable. Even if the correct amount of coal and water in the tender could be gauged so as to give a centrally balanced engine it would still have been impossible to turn a McDonnell engine on a 42ft 0in turntable because the flanges of the front and rear wheels would have overhung the turntable rails and fouled the fixed rails at each end. The *Working Timetable Appendix* stated that a 42ft 6in turntable was required for a McDonnell 4-4-0, but at the time the engines were built the majority of NER turntables were only 42ft 0in diameter! Consequently some engines were fitted with Fletcher tenders to reduce the wheelbase.

The change in driving position also caused some confusion, especially where a driver had habitually stopped by a mark on the right-hand side of the line, which was essential if the platform was on the left. With a right-hand platform and a left-hand drive engine the position was reversed and the drivers had to find new marks!

The Gateshead-built engines were put to stock at a figure of £3,000 each, and although Hawthorn & Company were paid £2,951 for each engine they built they were put to stock at £2,925 each.

Over the years a number of changes took place on these engines. First to go were the McDonnell chimneys, soon replaced by the Worsdell pattern. The uncovered Ramsbottom safety valves disappeared when Worsdell boilers replaced the originals. The cab side sheets were extended to provide better protection for the crew; originally the rear edge of the side sheet swept down in a curve, a noticeable feature being a handrail parallel to the curve and right at the crew's eye level! As modified the side sheet came down vertically at the extremity of the cab roof, and then curved to the horizontal. The curved handrail was replaced by a straight vertical handrail — but still at eye level! The front spectacles were rectangular, with the longer sides vertical.

Gravity sanders were fitted originally, so designed that the sand was deposited on the rail mid-way between the rear bogie wheel and the leading driving wheel, where it could easily be blown away before the wheel ever reached it! Later steam (or air?) sanders

Right: Class 38. More common are views of McDonnell engines in original condition except for the Worsdell chimney, as in this view of 180, in T. W. Worsdell livery. The photograph was taken at York (Clifton) shed c1890; the coal stage in the background was demolished c1915 when the shed was extended and a new roundhouse section added to the 1878 building. A new coal stage was built further north in the shed yard but this was superseded by a mechanical coaling plant in the 1930s. / *LPC*

Below right: Class 38. Sixteen engines were built at Gateshead Works in 1884, and twelve by R. & W. Hawthorn (Nos 1492-1503) in 1884/5. The Hawthorn engines differed in that the running plate over the connecting rods did not sweep upwards as much as on the Gateshead engines. The framing at the front end also differed. This is 1495 of the Hawthorn batch. / *J. W. Armstrong collection*

were fitted, delivering very close to the wheel. One engine, No 1500, is known to have had an additional sandbox on each side mounted on the running plate between the driving wheel splashers, to deliver sand to the back of the leading driver for tender-first running.

Another oddity was 1318 which, in its final days, had a cab with a single window on each side. This engine was stationed at Darlington (Bank Top) and used to work the Stores Vans train, going as far as Whitby to the south-east, and over Stainmore to Tebay and Penrith in the north-west. The improved cab was fitted to give the crew better protection over the exposed sections of the line.

Some engines had a splasher behind the rear bogie wheel, whilst on the splashers of the leading driving wheels NORTH EASTERN RAILWAY was engraved in the brass beading. At least two engines (158 and 1496) lost their rectangular numberplates and received in place oval plates of the Worsdell pattern.

When McDonnell left the North Eastern there was an order outstanding at Gateshead Works for eight 4-4-0s. The Locomotive Committee, under the chairmanship of Henry Tennant, which took charge in the interim period before T. W. Worsdell arrived, decided that work on these eight engines should not go ahead, even though some material was in hand, and on 5 February 1885 it was decided that they should appear as 0-6-0T engines. Consequently they were turned out in the last five months of 1885 and known as Class 8; this classification had nothing to do with the fact that there were eight engines, but was the lowest running number carried by one of the engines. However, its significance was lost in 1914 when this engine was renumbered 467 to make way for one of the Shildon electric locomotives. The 0-6-0Ts showed their McDonnell ancestry in their uncovered Ramsbottom safety valves and wing plates to the smokebox. On the LNER they became Class J74 and lasted until 1931, whereas only one 4-4-0 lasted into LNER days — and then not long enough to receive an LNER classification.

For many years the 4-4-0 engines ran with two sets of guard iron — one pair on the front of the bogie and the other pair on the main frames, but those on the bogie were eventually removed.

Right: Class 38 No 1495 preparing to leave Carlisle on a Newcastle train, with Carlisle No 5 signalbox in the background. The engine has received a Worsdell boiler. / *LPC*

Below right: Class 38. No 112 in Scarborough (Central) station c1912. The practice of putting a spare lamp on the same bracket as that showing the headcode was common on the NER. The engine has been converted to right-hand drive from the standard McDonnell left-hand position — the rod and crank can be seen behind the leading splasher. Note Fletcher tender fitted to some of these engines to allow them to turn on a 42ft turntable. The engines with a McDonnell tender required a 42ft 6in turntable. / *W. L. Good*

Class 38 Built at Darlington

Engine	*Built*	*Worsdell Boiler*	*Withdrawn*	*Last Shed*	*Notes*
38	10/84	5/97	2/15	Gateshead	1
112	10/84	9/98	3/15	Middlesbrough	1
126	12/84	4/96	11/21	York	
158	12/84	10/99	10/21	York	1
180	5/84	8/96	10/19	Malton	3
186	4/84	12/95	3/15	Selby	3
231	11/84	8/98	1/15	Selby	
234	12/84	1/97	7/15	Leeds	1
281	12/84	2/97	2/23	York	1
385	8/84	11/97	4/15	Selby	3
426	6/84	6/96	2/15	Hull	
500	9/84	12/95	2/17	Darlington	
576	7/84	6/96	3/18	Gateshead	3
664	6/84	2/97	6/20	Malton	4
1318	2/84	8/95	12/20	Darlington	4
1331	9/84	4/97	4/20	Gateshead	

Built by R. & W. Hawthorn & Co

Engine	*Built*	*Worsdell Boiler*	*Withdrawn*	*Last Shed*	*Notes*
1492	10/84	4/97	3/15	Hull	
1493	10/84	4/96	4/16	Hull	
1494	11/84	1/00	5/15	Gateshead	
1495	12/84	8/96	1/15	Blaydon	
1496	12/84	12/97	3/21	Hull	
1497	1/85	9/98	4/17	Hull	
1498	2/85	5/99	1/15	Hull	
1499	2/85	8/00	7/19	Hull	
1500	3/85	11/96	12/21	Middlesbrough	
1501	3/85	12/97	11/20	Middlesbrough	
1502	4/85	8/98	5/17	Selby	2
1503	4/85	5/97	6/15	Scarborough	1

Notes

1 Fitted with Fletcher tender
2 Tender used as water carrier at Hull subsequent to withdrawal
3 Fitted with vacuum brake (in addition to normal Westinghouse)
4 Tender sold to Harton Coal Company subsequent to withdrawal

BOVRIL

CLASS

Above: Class 38. No 281, still with left-hand drive, at Leeds (New) c1900; the engine has a Worsdell boiler (fitted in February 1897). NORTH EASTERN RAILWAY is engraved on the brass beading of the driving wheel splasher. This was the last McDonnell 4-4-0 to remain in service and the only one to become LNER property; it was withdrawn in February 1923. / *LPC*

Above right: Class 38. No 1318 often used in the Darlington area as the Stores Train engine and for this duty it was provided with a single-window cab to give additional shelter to the crew on their trips over Stainmore Summit. / *Author's collection*

Right: Class 38. A Whitby-bound train at Glaisdale, with the River Esk in the background. / *Author's collection*

1318
N. E. R.

5 Class 901 – Rebuilt as 4-4-0 1907

One class of North Eastern 4-4-0 was brought into existence by the rebuilding of a Fletcher Class 901 2-4-0 originally built by Neilson & Company in 1873. This was No 933, which in 1907 was fitted with a leading bogie, a new non-standard boiler and, most surprisingly, a Worsdell double side window cab. The result was a good looking 4-4-0 but its appearance was marred by the Fletcher tender it retained, with springs above the running plate. By all accounts the engine was not very successful and it was withdrawn after a life of only seven years in its new form.

Slightly larger driving wheels were fitted — 7ft 1¼in against the original 7ft 0in — with bogie wheels 3ft 7¼in. The driving wheels were 9ft 1in apart and the bogie wheelbase was 6ft 7in, giving a wheelbase of 22ft 6in. The boiler was 10ft 6in long and 4ft 10in diameter, with a total heating surface of 1,199.2sq ft. The grate area was 19sq ft. The driving wheels were the same size as on the M and Q engines, and the bogie wheels were the standard 3ft 7¼in, but why a 6ft 7in bogie when the standard was 6ft 6in? And why a 4ft 10in boiler when the Class R boiler was so close at 4ft 9in? Boiler pressure was officially quoted as 160lb and 180lb!

This was the first North Eastern 4-4-0 with separate splashers, after twenty years of continuous splashers, but separate splashers appeared again in the following year on the R1 engines. The engine numberplate was affixed in the centre of the rear splasher, which was outlined with brass beading; all previous 4-4-0s had their plates in the centre of the continuous splashers, the right-hand plate being on a hinged mounting to allow access to the Westinghouse brake pump. The Company's small coat-of-arms was carried on the leading splashers. At first 933 was stationed at Selby, where it worked the following diagram:

	arr	*dep*
Selby	——	7.14am (6.03am ex-Hull)
Church Fenton	7.34am	8.05am (via Wetherby)
Leeds	9.14am	9.50am (via Wetherby)
Hull	12.32pm	2.05pm (Liverpool train)
Selby (Change crews)	2.45pm	2.50pm
Leeds	3.21pm	4.23pm
South Milford	4.52pm	5.05pm
Leeds	5.31pm	5.45pm
Selby	6.28pm	7.09pm
Hull (engine utilised for shunting)	8.16pm	11.25pm
Selby	12.19am	——

In 1913 No 933 was transferred to Darlington and out-stationed at Barnard Castle, where it is reputed to have done little work; it was withdrawn from Barnard Castle on 8 July 1914.

Although not falling within the scope of this work it may be mentioned that another Class 901 2-4-0 (No 167) was rebuilt at the same time, although in this case it remained a 2-4-0. This engine was fitted with another odd-sized boiler, 4ft 8¾in dia and 10ft 3in long pitched 15½in higher than normal on Class 901, necessitating a short chimney and a low dome which completely altered its appearance. Driving wheels 7ft 1¼in dia were fitted. Although differing completely from the original engines, and from each other, both 933 and 167 remained Class 901. No 167 continued to run until 3 May 1920, when it was withdrawn from Scarborough shed.

Class 901

Engine	*Built*	*Rebuilt as 4-4-0*	*Withdrawn*	*Last shed*
933	12/73*	1907	7/14	Barnard Castle

* Built by Neilson Reid & Co

Above: Class 901. Fletcher 2-4-0 No 933 at Darlington (Bank Top) shed c1900. / *Author's collection*

Below: Class 901. In 1907 No 933 was rebuilt as a 4-4-0 and although a handsome engine its appearance was ruined by the use of a Fletcher tender. After rebuilding it was sent to Selby shed, before moving to Darlington in 1913. It was outstationed at Barnard Castle and is reputed to have been stored there, out of use, and out of sight, before being withdrawn in July 1914. / *Author's collection*

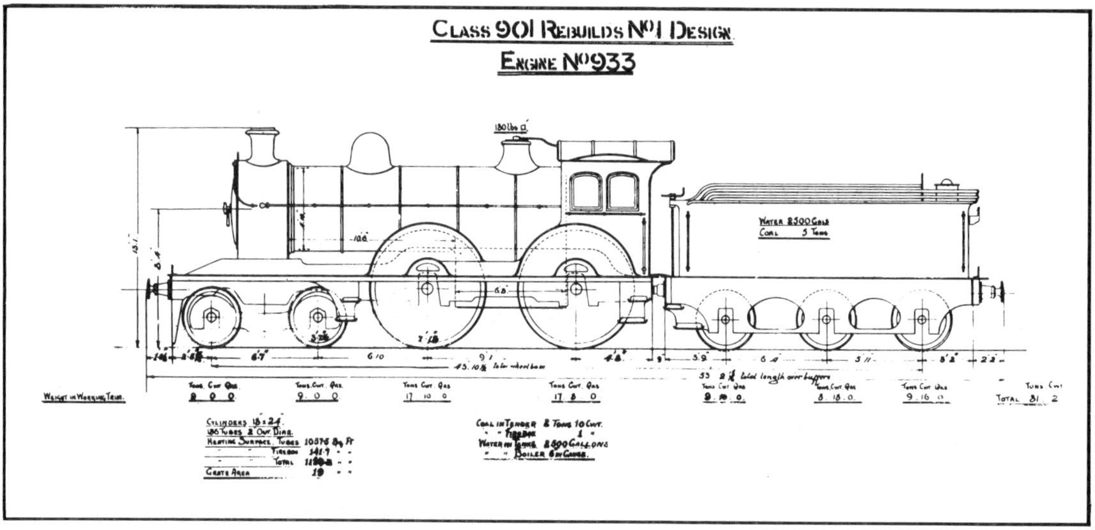

Above: Class 901. Drawing of 933. / *Author's collection*

Below: Class 901. No 167 was also rebuilt in 1907, producing another unique NER engine, which at first was stationed at Darlington, although it was transferred to Scarborough about 1917 before being withdrawn in May 1920. / *Author's collection*

6 Class D – T. W. Worsdell 2-4-0 Introduced 1886

Although T. W. Worsdell designed and built two-cylinder compound 4-4-0 engines for the Great Eastern Railway, his first passenger design for the North Eastern was a compound 2-4-0 turned out in November 1886 and it seems likely that this decision recognised the North Eastern men's dislike of the McDonnell 4-4-0 design. However, after this sole 2-4-0 Worsdell produced seven months later the first of a series of 20 4-4-0 engines, ten of which were compounds and ten were simples. The compounds were identical with the 2-4-0 engine except for the wheel arrangement and weight.

For some reason as yet undiscovered another 2-4-0 compound was built in December 1888, similar to the original engine but having Smith's patent piston valves, one 7in dia for the high-pressure cylinder, and two 5½in dia for the low pressure. The latter were placed side by side above the cylinder and actuated by one rod connected to each valve spindle. The cylinders had fixed to them at each end a 2in spring-loaded relief valve to allow any trapped water to escape. A further 15 compound 4-4-0s were built in 1890/1.

Worsdell's first design for the North Eastern was a simple 2-4-2T (Class A) soon followed by 0-6-2T (Class B) and 0-6-0 (Class C) compounds, which eventually totalled 202 engines. However, many of these were actually built after T. W. Worsdell had retired and been succeeded by his brother Wilson. As with the 4-4-0s, simple engines were built simultaneously for comparison purposes, comprising 11 Class B1 0-6-2T and 10 Class C1 0-6-0.

The two compound 2-4-0s were both rebuilt with a leading bogie, converted to simples, and reclassified F1 in October 1896.

Class D

Engine	*Built*	*Rebuilt as 4-4-0 Class F1*	*Superheated*	*Withdrawn*	*Last shed*
340	12/88	10/96	8/15	12/33	Botanic Gardens
1324	11/86	10/96	2/17	2/30	Carlisle

Class D. No 1324 prepared for display at the Golden Jubilee Exhibition held at Newcastle in 1887. Note the Worsdell-von Borries plate at the base of the smokebox. / *Author's collection*

Top: Class F1. No 1324 running as a superheated 4-4-0 in LNER days, photographed at Carlisle. The safety valve base was to a non-standard design used on some North Eastern engines fitted with Ross 'pop' safety valves. / *J. J. Cunningham*

Above: Class D. No 340, built two years after 1324, was fitted with piston valves. Tail rods to the pistons necessitated extended frames and running plate at the front end. Photographed at Carlisle (London Road) shed c1894. / *Author's collection*

Below: Class F1. No 340 in its final form as a 4-4-0 with superheated boiler, photographed at Hull (Botanic Gardens) shed c1932; it was withdrawn in 1933. / *R. H. Inness*

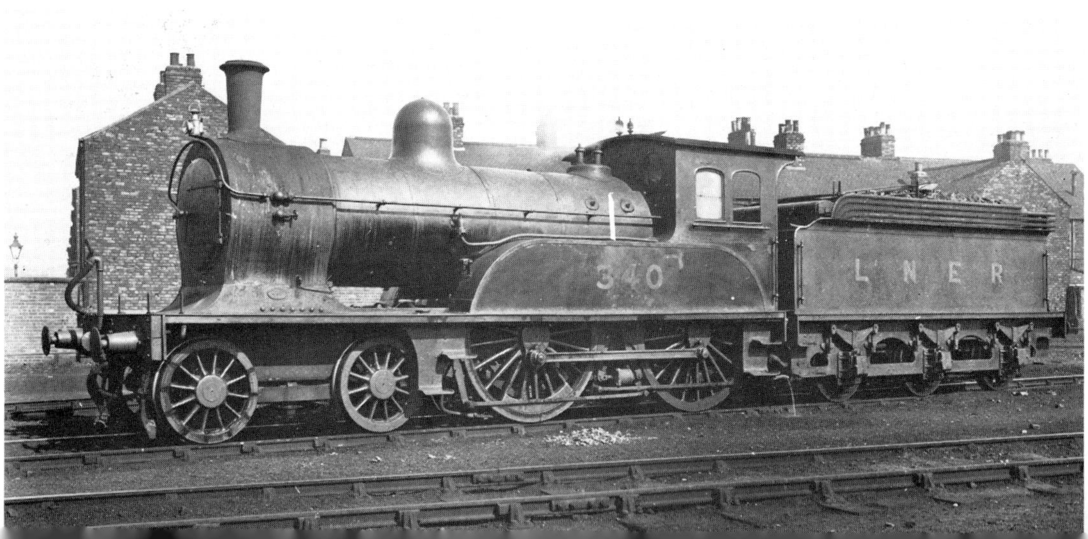

7 Classes F & F1 – T. W. Worsdell 4-4-0 Introduced 1887

T. W. Worsdell's first North Eastern 4-4-0 appeared from Gateshead works in June 1887; this was a two-cylinder compound engine and a further nine were built before the end of the year, together with 10 simples:

Class F	June 1887: 18, 42, 115
(Compound)	November 1887: 117, 355, 514, 779
	December 1887: 1, 663, 684
Class F1	November 1887: 230, 673, 777, 803
(Simple)	December 1887: 85, 96, 154, 194, 808, 1137

A further 15 compounds, 1532-1546, were built in 1890/1, also at Gateshead.

The design was generally similar to the 2-4-0 engine of Class D (1324) introduced in November 1886, the only difference being the use of a bogie instead of a single carrying axle. The compound engines were subsequently rebuilt as simples (and fitted with piston valves) and the simple engines were also fitted with piston valves. All engines were fitted with superheated boilers between 1913 and 1920.

On his Great Eastern 4-4-0s Worsdell used a continuous splasher over the coupled wheels, together with a plain cab and a stovepipe chimney, and although a similar splasher was used on the North Eastern engines the cab was transformed into a double side window version — used on all North Eastern tender engines built subsequently — and the chimney became a handsome cast iron pattern with a top lip.

Mr Worsdell's decision to try compounding on the Great Eastern was, so we are told, taken as he was casting about for means of reducing the working expenses of the line; and that when the first two-cylinder compound engine was tried out on the road 'it would sometimes stop with the high-pressure crank at the dead point when, of course, the engine would neither go one way or the other'. One solution to this problem was to arrange for steam to be admitted to the low-pressure valve chest at the driver's discretion, but 'in practice the drivers always preferred to reverse the engine first if it would not start at once — before resorting to the auxiliary valve'. Consequently a starting valve was fitted to allow steam direct from the boiler into the steamchest of the LP cylinder, in conjunction with an intercepting valve. In practice if the engine would not start the intercepting valve was closed by the driver to prevent steam from the starting valve reaching the HP cylinder, and he then turned on the auxiliary steam and opened the regulator. The first exhaust from the HP cylinder opened the intercepting valve for normal compound working, and the auxiliary steam was turned off.

By the time Worsdell was turning out compound engines for the North Eastern the starting equipment had been modified so that only one handle was required. By pulling back a small spring-loaded lever on the front plate of the cab the starting valve was opened, allowing steam from the boiler to pass to the LP cylinder, on the way operating a piston which closed the intercepting valve to prevent steam from reaching the HP cylinder. As soon as the engine moved the driver released the lever, thus closing the auxiliary steam supply, and with the first exhaust of the HP cylinder the intercepting valve was blown open to allow normal compound working.

As usual with new designs the new 4-4-0 engines were soon put to work on the company's main trains — in this case the East Coast Joint Stock services which the North Eastern powered between York and Edinburgh, with a change of engines at Newcastle. However, it was the Races to Edinburgh of 1888 which brought the Class F engines into prominence, with Driver Bob Nicholson's 130 minutes for the 124 miles from Newcastle to Edinburgh on 31 August 1888.

The spell of these 4-4-0 engines on the main North Eastern expresses lasted for six years, because in 1893 they were rapidly eclipsed by Wilson Worsdell's Class M1 engines. The T. W. Worsdell engines were then used for many years on the more important branch line services such as Newcastle-Carlisle, Leeds-Hull, Leeds-Scarborough, Hull-Scarborough etc. By the end of World War I the North Eastern had 72 Atlantics for main line services, and as traffic decreased the various types of 4-4-0s were downgraded and the Class F engines, as the oldest, were relegated to minor branch services such as Hull-Hornsea, Hull-Withernsea, Harrogate-York, Selby-

Bridlington, and the less important Hull-Leeds and Hull-Doncaster trains. In the north they appeared on slow trains on the main line, and also on the Amble branch.

The final fifteen Class F compounds were built after Wilson Worsdell had succeeded his brother as Locomotive Superintendent of the North Eastern, but he did not share his brother's liking for compounding, and the directors forming the Locomotive Committee were also uncertain about the advantage, or otherwise, of the system. Consequently on 5 October 1893 the Committee instructed Wilson Worsdell to arrange for a full report 'with reference to the working of Compound Engines compared with the working of other Classes of Engines on the North Eastern Railway'. Thorough and extensive trials were carried

out on passenger and goods engines by two of Worsdell's assistants, Vincent Raven and Ramsey Kendal, and their 20-page *PRIVATE AND CONFIDENTIAL* report was forwarded to Sir Lowthian Bell, the Chairman of the Locomotive Committee. It included tables of dimensions and fuel consumption and came to the conclusion: 'the argument at present to be deduced from the working of these (compound) engines does not enable us to report favourably upon this class as compared with the ordinary type'.

The findings of Raven and Kendal eventually led to the conversion of the compound engines to simples and with Class F the first to be done was 663 in January 1900, and the last was 1545 in November 1905. At the same time the Joy valve gear was replaced by Stephenson link motion and the slide valves by piston valves.

The next major modification was the fitting of superheaters to all the engines of the class, commencing with Nos 117 and 684 in September 1913, taking until June 1920 to complete the task, when 1532 was altered. The ten engines built as simples (Class F1) were similarly treated, being fitted with Stephenson gear and piston valves between February 1903 (85) and June 1911 (803); superheating followed between August 1914 (96) and July 1919 (1137).

The Worsdell cab layout used on these 4-4-0s was to remain the standard until the end of the North Eastern, and even beyond; it can still be seen in use on the North Yorkshire Moors Railway, where P3 0-6-0 No 2392 and T2 0-8-0 No 2238 follow the Worsdell tradition although both were built in the Raven era. However, they differ in that whereas the passenger engines had screw reverse the goods engines had lever reverse (2392) and steam reverse (2238). A 4-4-0 cab can be inspected on one of the preserved engines in the National Railway Museum, No 1621.

However, as I have explained elsewhere, Worsdell and Raven cabs were not as spacious as they appeared. To start with, the back end of the boiler projected some 15in into the cab, and then there were the boiler mountings taking up about 9in. A large metal box splasher with a wooden seat on top covered the coupled wheels and this ran the length of the cab on each side, although on the driver's side more than half the forward end was taken up by the reversing screw. On the fireman's side there was no obstruction and two people could easily sit side by side. The trouble was that your back was then to the side window and you had to turn through 90 degrees to see out of the front spectacle — but anyone sitting close up to the boiler could only be seen with difficulty from outside the engine, especially if a thick railway jacket was judiciously hung to obscure the view — as I discovered when I had my first express footplate journey when a schoolboy!

Anyone standing on the floor of the cab could not see out of the front spectacles, and long footboxes (or footstands) about 12in wide and 12in high were built

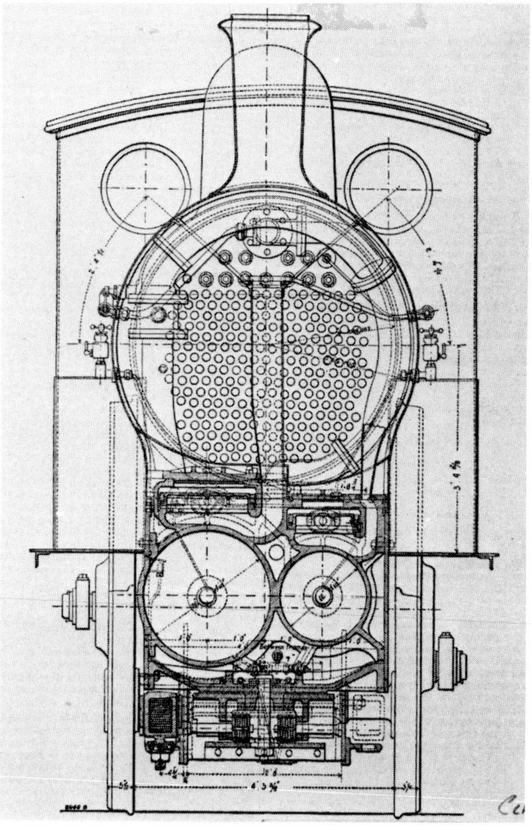

Above left: Class F. T. W. Worsdell's first 4-4-0 design for the North Eastern was a 2-cylinder compound with Joy's valve gear. The engine chosen for the official view was 684, one of the first batch of 10 compounds built in 1887. / *Author's collection*

Left: Class F. Also from the first batch was 779, seen here at Edinburgh (Waverley), with the old North Bridge in the background. The engine is in its original T. W. Worsdell livery and it was obviously photographed soon after building. Note the slide valve covers at different levels below the smokebox door, so arranged to suit the 18in (high pressure) cylinder and the 26in (low pressure) cylinder. / *LPC*

Right: Class F. The low pressure cylinder protruded through the frame on the right-hand side of the engine. / *Author's collection*

Above: Class F1. No 1 is seen here after being rebuilt as a 2-cylinder simple in December 1903, in Wilson Worsdell livery with the large crest on the tender. The loading classification, T4, is below the number plate. This engine was renumbered 356 in 1914, bringing to an end a nine-year duplication as the number was also carried by one of the electric locomotives used on the Newcastle Quayside branch. / *Author's collection*

Bottom right: Class F1. Another rebuild — this time 117, seen on the Stores Train, which called at all stations on the North Eastern system to dispense items used in the day-to-day running of the railway. / *Author's collection*

along the cab, inside each coupled wheel splasher, leaving a well about 2ft wide in the centre of the cab, with the firehole door at the leading end, and the fall-plate between engine and tender at the other.

The wheel type of reversing handle was fitted originally but this was later changed for a new type consisting of a bar about 3in wide, 1½in thick, and about 18in long, with a handle at each end. One handle was fixed, but the other was spring loaded and could be moved through 45deg to disengage the gear from the notched quadrant plate surrounding the screw. The driver could then alter the cut-off as required and lock the gear in the desired position by clicking the handle back into place.

Another refinement fitted in North Eastern cabs was the 'blinder' on the firehole door. Metal side sheets with a curved top were fitted vertically on either side of the door and across these went two sheets hinged in the middle. The top sheet was also hinged to a rod running across the two vertical sheets, parallel to the boiler back plate. In the dropped position the two sheets hung down, following the arc of the side sheets, obscuring the glare from the firehole door and cutting out annoying reflections in the front spectacles. In the raised position the two sheets were lifted and folded about the centre hinge, so that the bottom edge of the lower sheet rested in grooves on either side sheet, with both sheets almost vertical and the centre hinge at the top.

All these engines were fitted with Westinghouse brake when built, and in addition 1532-1546 were built with vacuum ejectors for working vacuum braked stock; Nos 777 and 808 also received vacuum ejectors in June 1899. Under the LNER programme for the standardisation of the vacuum brake nine engines received vacuum ejectors in 1928/9, but the remaining nine (18, 42, 96, 117, 154, 355, 514, 684 and 803) still only had Westinghouse brake when withdrawn. The two 2-4-0 engines, 340 and 1324, were fitted with vacuum ejectors when they were rebuilt as 4-4-0s in October 1896.

Allocation of Class D22 Engines February 1923

Alnmouth	1	18
Bridlington	7	115, 117, 230, 514, 684, 1536, 1539
Carlisle	3	154, 355, 1324
Gateshead	1	1546
Hull-Botanic Gardens	11	42, 85, 96, 194, 340, 777, 803, 1137, 1534, 1540, 1543
Hull-Springhead	2	808, 1538
Scarborough	4	356, 779, 1541, 1542
Selby	5	673, 1532, 1535, 1537, 1544
Starbeck	2	1533, 1545
Waskerley	1	663
Total	37	

Class F Built at Gateshead

Engine	*Built*	*Rebuilt as Simple (F1)*	*Superheated*	*Withdrawn*	*Last shed*
1/356	12/87	12/03	3/20	3/32	Botanic Gardens
18	6/87	3/95	10/16	1/29	Gateshead
42	6/87	10/04	2/15	5/30	Scarborough
115	6/87	9/04	3/14	12/33	Bradford (LMS)
117	11/87	11/03	9/13	3/29	Botanic Gardens
355	11/87	10/01	9/15	1/30	Carlisle
514	11/87	5/00	3/14	2/29	Botanic Gardens
663	12/87	1/00	10/19	10/32	Botanic Gardens
684	12/87	2/03	9/13	6/30	Selby
779	11/87	10/02	8/14	2/30	Scarborough
1532	12/90	9/05	6/20	4/30	Botanic Gardens
1533	12/90	7/05	4/18	9/31	Starbeck
1534	12/90	12/04	4/18	10/29	Selby
1535	12/90	2/05	9/14	7/33	Selby
1536	12/90	11/04	1/14	9/31	Botanic Gardens
1537	12/90	1/05	4/16	11/35	Selby
1538	12/90	5/01	6/18	6/33	Scarborough
1539	12/90	3/04	12/13	2/30	Botanic Gardens
1540	12/90	7/05	7/18	10/29	Botanic Gardens
1541	12/90	5/05	2/20	9/34	Starbeck
1542	12/90	6/05	4/20	7/33	Stockton
1543	12/90	10/05	1/17	8/32	Botanic Gardens
1544	12/90	3/05	2/16	8/29	Selby
1545	4/91	11/05	3/16	12/31	Starbeck
1546	4/91	4/01	12/16	1/35	Botanic Gardens

Class F1 Built at Gateshead

85	12/87	—	4/16	10/32	Botanic Gardens
96	12/87	—	8/14	4/27	Botanic Gardens
154	12/87	—	3/17	2/30	Carlisle
194	12/87	—	12/15	4/30	Botanic Gardens
230	11/87	—	2/18	2/30	Botanic Gardens
673	11/87	—	2/16	10/33	Selby
777	11/87	—	11/14	5/35	Waskerley
803	11/87	—	1/18	5/29	Botanic Gardens
808	12/87	—	3/16	2/30	Stockton
1137	12/87	—	7/19	11/29	Botanic Gardens

L N E R
356

Above: Class F1. No 777 was an engine originally built as a simple in 1887, seen here at Darlington (North Road) station in the 1930s on a Darlington (Bank Top) to Blackhill train. Part of North Road station is now used as a railway museum devoted mainly to Stockton & Darlington and North Eastern items. / *J. W. Armstrong*

Above left: Class F1. No 356, originally 1, is seen at Scarborough shed in the 1920s, in LNER livery and superheated. By this time the engine had become LNER Class D22. / *W. H. Whitworth*

Left: Class F1. No 1545, a Starbeck engine, leaves York for Harrogate at the head of a train of four North Eastern Bain clerestory coaches. / *H. L. Salmon*

Right: Class F1. To work the Blackhill-Darlington service No 777 was stationed at Waskerley shed, and it was from there that it was withdrawn from service in May 1935. On 1 June it was photographed in the Scrap Yard at Darlington awaiting cutting up — only just across the road from the previous photograph. / *H. C. Casserley*

Below: Class F1. During the winter months engines were often put into store, such as 1546, seen in the former Hull & Barnsley locomotive works at Springhead (Hull) in the 1930s. / *T. E. Rounthwaite*

8 Class G1 – T. W. Worsdell 4-4-0 Introduced 1887

At the same time as the major batch of F and F1 4-4-0 engines was being built at Gateshead (in November and December 1887) a series of 20 2-4-0s was commenced at Darlington Works. These were two-cylinder simple engines intended for branch line services, and they used the same boiler and cylinders as T. W. Worsdell's initial design for the North Eastern, the Class A 2-4-2T. They were put to work in the Southern Division, running mainly in the area bounded by Hull-Leeds-Scarborough.

The original classification of these engines has often been wrongly quoted, being said to be Class G when built as 2-4-0s and G1 when rebuilt as 4-4-0s. The fact is that they were Class G1 when built, following the precedent set by classes B1, C1 and F1 in having a figure 1 suffix for the non-compound engines. In this case Class G was left blank as there were no compounds although, as explained in the Introduction, the figure 1 suffix was abolished in June 1914, by which time all had been rebuilt as 4-4-0s. During the period from December 1900 to August 1904, when they were being rebuilt as 4-4-0s both original and rebuilt engines were Class G1.

When these engines were rebuilt as 4-4-0s they were fitted with piston valves and their Joy valve gear was replaced by Stephenson link motion. At the same time they received 18in cylinders in place of the original 17in although one engine, 328, had received 18in cylinders in July 1899 whilst still a 2-4-0, presumably retaining its Joy gear until it was rebuilt as a 4-4-0 five years later.

Superheating of this class commenced in January 1913 and proceeded rapidly, so that 18 engines had been done by the end of 1914, and the remaining pair were superheated in 1915 and 1916. When rebuilt with a superheated boiler and an extended smokebox, seven engines received new and deeper frames based on Raven practice; these frames continued at the same height both behind and in front of the smokebox, with the front portion eventually curving down to running plate level just behind the buffer-beam. In later days this allowed lifting holes to be provided. The engines concerned were Nos 214, 222, 337, 472, 521, 679 and 1120.

Below: Class G1. The official photograph of 274 in grey livery: the engine was built at Gateshead in 1887. / *Author's collection*

As 4-4-0s they continued on the same duties — Hull-Leeds, Hull-Scarborough, Scarborough-York, Whitby-York, Harrogate-Leeds, and Harrogate-York: it was not until the 1920s that any notable transfers were made. The building of 15 Gresley Pacifics for the North Eastern Area demoted Raven Atlantics which, in turn, displaced Class R 4-4-0s, and so on down the ranks. Thus as Hull received larger engines the D23 4-4-0s at the bottom of the ladder were redundant, but fortunately at the same time engines were required to replace the rapidly disappearing Fletcher and Tennant 2-4-0s on the Darlington-Kirkby Stephen-Tebay and Penrith services and the D23 engines filled the gap for some years until they too were put on the withdrawal list. In fact when withdrawal commenced in 1929 there were 14 of the class at work in the Darlington and Kirkby Stephen area, although they also appeared on Darlington-Richmond and Darlington-Saltburn services. At this time Darlington had 8, Barnard Castle 3, Middleton-in-Teesdale 1, and Kirkby Stephen 2. The remaining six were divided between Waskerley, Malton, Tweedmouth, Duns, Starbeck and Bradford (Manningham). The Waskerley engine worked twice daily to Darlington on the Blackhill service; the Malton engine worked to Whitby; the Tweedmouth and Duns engines worked on the former North Eastern and North British border branches, the North British shed at Duns having come under the control of Tweedmouth after the formation of the LNER. The Starbeck engine worked services around Harrogate, and the Bradford engine worked to York and back daily.

Fortunately detailed costs survive of many classes of engines built at Darlington and these contain fascinating items, such as in 1888 when a Class G1 chimney weighed 225lb and cost 18s 1d (90p), with fixing bolts, nuts and washers costing 7d (3p). The glass for the four cab windows cost 15s 5d (77p), and

Below: Class G1. The first to be built was 557, seen here in its original T. W. Worsdell livery. / *Author's collection*

the two circular spectacle glasses, 17in in diameter, cost 4s 8d (23p). The cab required 105ft super of teak, 30ft of 1in mahogany, and 3ft of 11in x 3in deal costing altogether £5 6s 5d (£5 32p). The cast brass beading for the driving wheels splashers cost £1 7s 7d (£1 38p) the pair. The four steel driving wheels cost £109 15s 5d (£109 77p) complete with tyres, and the crank axle £65 2s 7d (£65 13p). The 26ft x 4ft by 1in frames cost £35 1s 1d (£35 5p) the pair. The cylinder block was £27 19s 11d (£27 99½p) and the two cast iron pistons and steel rods £3 4s 6d (£3 22½p). A set of Westinghouse brake fittings cost £65 5s (£65 25p).

The above prices are all for materials only and the total for engine and tender amounted to £1,252 7s 7d (£1,252 38p). Machining the parts and erecting the engine and tender cost £755 5s 6d (£755 27½p), giving a total cost of £2,007 13s 1d (£2,007 65p) made up as follows:

	Materials			*Wages*			*Total*		
	£	s	d	£	s	d	£	s	d
Boiler and firebox	288	16	6	77	5	0	366	1	6
Smokebox, platform etc	58	6	7	89	1	6	147	8	1
Wheels, springs, frames etc	335	10	2	80	0	4	415	10	6
Cylinders, motion, axleboxes	140	15	0	198	12	4	339	7	4
Injectors, valves etc	59	10	2	24	5	8	83	15	10
Clothing, cleading, painting	36	16	4	49	15	0	86	11	4
Westinghouse brake	80	10	5	24	2	10	104	13	3
Erecting engine	—	—	—	55	10	3	55	10	3
Cost of engine	1,000	5	2	598	12	11	1,598	18	1
Cost of tender	252	2	5	156	12	7	408	15	0
Total cost of engine and tender	1,252	7	7	755	5	6	2,007	13	1

In addition to the cost of materials and labour there were the general expenses of the works and the complete locomotives were put to stock at £2,591 each.

Incidentally, the piece-work rate for painting the engine was £5, plus £3 4s 2d time work, and the tender £5 plus £1 2s 6d time work. Both were given three coats of paint and four of varnish. The engine required 8⁹⁄₁₀ quarts of varnish and tender 9½ quarts!

Class G1 Built at Darlington

Engine	*Built*	*Rebuilt as 4-4-0*	*Superheated*	*Withdrawn*	*Last shed*
23	12/87	4/01	2/13	8/29	Waskerley
214	10/88	5/03	9/14	5/30	Malton
217	10/88	9/01	4/14	8/31	Middleton-in-Teesdale
222	6/88	8/01	9/14	12/30	Barnard Castle
223	6/88	6/01	9/14	4/33	Barnard Castle
258	4/88	3/02	5/14	11/31	Starbeck
274	12/87	7/04	3/16	12/30	Darlington
328	4/88	8/04	6/14	10/31	Bradford (LMS)
337	6/88	8/04	2/14	8/33	Barnard Castle
372	10/88	6/03	4/13	12/30	Darlington
472	11/88	6/03	9/13	11/30	Darlington
521	6/88	2/01	11/14	12/30	Darlington
557	11/87	12/00	1/13	1/31	Darlington
675	12/87	5/04	3/14	3/20	Barnard Castle
676	12/87	5/04	4/14	1/30	Barnard Castle
677	12/87	5/02	11/13	12/33	Kirkby Stephen
678	11/87	7/02	1/14	12/33	Kirkby Stephen
679	12/87	5/03	7/13	1/31	Darlington
1107	11/88	12/01	2/13	6/30	Kirkby Stephen
1120	6/88	12/02	10/15	5/35	Bradford (LMS)

Above: Class G1. Rebuilding to 4-4-0s took place between 1900 and 1904, No 679's turn coming in May 1903. It is in the standard Wilson Worsdell green livery, with the large crest on the tender. / *Author's collection*

Centre left: Class G1. Superheating took place between 1913 and 1916 and this is 274 standing in Leeds (New) station in May 1920 on a train for Harrogate, when it was a Starbeck engine. / *J. W. Armstrong*

Below left: Class G1. The figure 1 suffix to the class was dropped in 1914 — probably the year in which the view was taken of 337 leaving Scarborough. / *W. L. Good*

Above right: Class G1. Another Starbeck engine was 328, although it was usually outstationed at the Midland shed at Manningham (Bradford). Here it is passing Poppleton Junction signalbox and diverging from the main line on to the Harrogate branch. Note the highly polished brass numberplate. / *H. L. Salmon*

Below right: Class G1. No 258, for long a Hull engine, moved north to the former North British shed at Duns in 1924, and later spent some time at Tweedmouth before returning south (to Starbeck) in 1929. It is seen here at Tweedmouth shed in May 1925, in the LNER lined black livery appropriate to North Eastern Area engines with 6ft $1\frac{1}{4}$in dia driving wheels; all other former North Eastern 4-4-0 engines were at first painted green by the LNER. / *Author's collection*

258

Above: Class G1. No 337, seen here at Darlington shed in June 1929, has gone into the new livery with the number on the splashers and LNER on the tender. It is one of the seven engines rebuilt with deeper frames: it also sports a capuchon chimney. / *R. H. Inness*

Below: Class G1. In addition to their duties on the Stainmore line these engines worked from Darlington to Saltburn and Richmond, and occasionally as far south as York. This is 223 on a Richmond-Darlington train at Croft Spa in April 1931, when it was stationed at Barnard Castle shed. / *W. Rogerson*

9 Class M – W. Worsdell 4-4-0 Introduced 1893

Concurrently with the 20 M1 engines (of which the first appeared in December 1892) Wilson Worsdell built a single example with compound cylinders, which appeared in May 1893. This was No 1619 working on the two-cylinder Worsdell-von Borries system with the high pressure cylinder 20in dia by 26in stroke, and the low pressure cylinder 28in dia by 26in stroke, the object being to settle once and for all the superiority — or otherwise — of the compound system as far as the North Eastern was concerned. All other dimensions of the two types were identical except that the boiler pressure of the simple engines was 160lb and the compound 200lb. The compound was also 14cwt heavier.

No details have been located of any special trials to compare the two types and they warrant only a brief mention in the report prepared by Raven and Kendal. In 1893 six engines each worked five return trips between Newcastle and Edinburgh with the following results:

Engine	*Class*	*Wheel arrgt*	*Boiler Pressure*	*Average Load (vehicles)*	*Coal lb/mile*	*Water lb/lb of coal*	*Oil Pints/ 1,000 miles*
640	901	2-4-0	140	12.1	31.4	7.2	33.0
1471	1463	2-4-0	160	10.8	30.2	7.4	37.0
1624	M1	4-4-0	160	10.4	32.5	7.0	58.3
1521	J	4-2-2	175	10.8	34.1	7.0	62.9
1545	F	4-4-0	175	12.5	29.9	7.3	58.2
1619	M	4-4-0	200	10.6	29.2	7.2	57.5

Although on these figures 1619 came out marginally the best as far as coal consumption was concerned the figures are not sufficiently detailed to provide any worthwhile and conclusive results, the most notable feature in fact being the high lubricating oil consumption of the three compounds and the M1! However, on trials held at the same time with nine M1 4-4-0s working over the same route No 1624 showed an even higher oil consumption of 65.5 pints per 1,000 miles, with No 1625 weighing in with 82.0 pints, which works out at 20½ pints (say 2½ gallons) for a Newcastle-Edinburgh return trip!

Although No 1619 was the only compound built to the designs of Wilson Worsdell in the first decade of his reign at Gateshead he had in fact continued to build compounds to his brother's designs until December 1892 (Class C1) — and yet two years later, in January 1895, he made a start on rebuilding all the compounds to simples, although the time for rebuilding No 1619 did not arrive until August 1898. However, it was not just a case of fitting a new set of high pressure cylinders and converting from Joy to Stephenson gear as 1619 was fitted with a new boiler and converted to a three cylinder compound on W. M. Smith's system. This made a handsome looking engine, the only Worsdell 4-4-0 with outside cylinders, and the only Worsdell 4-4-0 not subsequently superheated. During its existence in its new form 1619 had only two boilers, and when the second wore out and superheating may have been carried out on a new boiler it was decided to withdraw the engine rather than go to the expense of providing a single non-standard boiler. Consequently 1619 was taken out of service in October 1930 and scrapped at North Road Works, Darlington; it had latterly been working from Bridlington shed in company with a small stud of M1 engines on turns to Hull, Scarborough and Leeds. No 1619 remained green to the end, with its number on the tender, amassing a mileage of 909,331.

In its original form No 1619 cost £3,267 compared with £3,110 each for its twenty simple sisters.

When built 1619 had the high pressure cylinder on the left hand side and the low pressure on the right, and as the centre lines of the cylinders were 12in on either side of the centre line of the engine, and the frames were 4ft apart, the 28in dia low pressure

Above: Class M. Wilson Worsdell's doubts about the success of his brother's compound engines led him to build one engine for comparison with similar simple engines. The compound was 1619, built at Gateshead in May 1893, with 7ft $1\frac{1}{4}$in dia driving wheels. The official photograph was taken at Jarrow Slake — seen in the background at low tide — and it well illustrates the lines of this engine. The pipe rising out of the tender carried away exhaust steam after it had passed through the water in the tender. / *Author's collection*

Below: Class M. Although the quality of this photograph makes it not really suitable for reproduction it has been included as it is a rare view of 1619 at work. It is believed to be working the return special train conveying journalists on a demonstration run of the first East Coast Joint Stock dining car train from London to Edinburgh and back on 22 July 1893. The location is Stannington, north of Newcastle. / *Author's collection*

Above: Class M. In 1898 No 1619 was rebuilt as a 3-cylinder compound on W. M. Smith's system. Again it was towed to Jarrow Slake for the official photograph — and again it was low tide! The tender was now fitted with a larger tank, the top of which was above the level of the two coal rails. / *Author's collection*

Below: Class M. When rebuilt 1619 was fitted with water tubes in the firebox, but these could not be reached for cleaning purposes. The unsuitability of this arrangement led to the boiler being fitted with a new firebox in 1900, and this time provision was made for examining and descaling the water tubes. Three inspection holes were provided on each side of the outer firebox, with the necessary covers hidden by domes or 'blisters' to maintain the green livery of the engine. This view of 1619 was taken at York, with the engine waiting to take over a northbound train due to arrive at No 14 platform outside the main wall of the station. / *Author's collection*

cylinder casting had to project through the frames on the right hand side. There was no space for the valves either between or above the cylinders and they had to be placed outside and, being higher than on the simple engines, the valve chests were covered by a large box casing on either side of the base of the smokebox. The four eccentrics of the Stephenson gear were placed between the cranks and a form of rocking gear had to be devised to transmit the motion to the outside valves.

The receiver for the steam exhausted from the high pressure cylinder was a 9in dia pipe running round the interior of the smokebox, which was of the extended pattern for this very reason. Extended smokeboxes of this type were also fitted to the simple engines so that they could easily be converted to compound engines if required, but in the event this was not necessary and the extended smokeboxes were removed, although restored years later when the M1 engines were superheated.

In the three cylinder version the low pressure cylinders were 20in dia by 24in stroke, placed outside the frames and supplied with steam via slide valves alongside but inside the frames. The 19in × 26in high pressure cylinder on the centre line of the engine received its steam by means of a Smith's 8¾in piston valve below the cylinder. The steamchests and passages between the high pressure cylinder and the two low pressure cylinders were sufficiently capacious to handle the high pressure exhaust steam without the need for the receiver pipe as used on the original two cylinder version.

By means of a reducing valve on the right hand side of the smokebox it was possible to allow live steam at a required pressure into the low pressure valve chests: this could give a slight increase in pressure to help the engine overcome a rising gradient and in this case the engine was said to be working 'semi-compound', or it could be steam at full boiler pressure and the engine then worked as a two cylinder simple, with the high pressure cylinder in equilibrium. Full compound working was resumed as soon as conditions allowed.

The high pressure crank was at an angle of 135deg to each of the low pressure cranks which were, therefore, at right angles, the object of this being to secure a uniform turning moment when the low pressure cylinders were performing all or a very large part of the work, and it also gave a more uniform exhaust from the blastpipe.

Externally 1619 differed from the other North Eastern 4-4-0s of the period in having the boiler clothing flush with the smokebox; and the splashers, instead of having a continuous brass beading, had each wheel arch outlined by a separate brass beading. Separate open sections were provided for the coupling rod ends, the rod itself being outside the connecting rod. The outside cylinders were partly above and partly below the running plate and this design was later followed on the V, V/09 and S2 engines.

Class M (Later Reclassified 3CC)

Engine	*Built*	*Rebuilt as 3-cyl compound*	*Withdrawn*	*Last Shed*
1619	5/93	8/98	10/30	Bridlington

Below: Class M. Until the 1920s No 1619 ran with a brass capped chimney, but in its final years it ran with a plain capuchon chimney. It was photographed at Selby in 1929, the year before it was withdrawn, working from Bridlington shed. On the right hand side of the engine its appearance was spoiled by the vacuum pipe running outside the bogie. / *R. H. Inness*

10 Class M1 – W. Worsdell 4-4-0 Introduced 1892

Wilson Worsdell's first design of 4-4-0 appeared late in 1892, when 1620 of Class M1 was turned out from Gateshead Works: a further 18 engines were built in 1893, and the twentieth, 1639, in 1894. A compound engine of similar dimensions, known as Class M and numbered 1619, appeared in 1893. When T. W. Worsdell had built simple and compound engines concurrently he had usually shown a marked preference for compounds, but in this case Wilson Worsdell's ratio was 1 compound to 20 simples! However, the compound was built on the Worsdell-von Borries two cylinder system as favoured by the elder Worsdell, and the simples were designed with extended smokeboxes so that they could more easily be converted to compounds if 1619 showed a marked superiority.

These new 4-4-0s were originally authorised by the directors on 18 February 1892 as 20 Class F1 engines, but this order was cancelled and they were re-ordered on 21 April 1892 as 21 M and M1 engines. They were notable as being the first British 4-4-0 engines to weigh more than 90 tons in working order.

Because of the 19in × 26in cylinders Wilson Worsdell decided to put the valve chests outside the frames, with the valves operated by rocking levers from inside Stephenson link motion, 1620-38 having slide valves and 1639 having Smith's patent piston valves. Both types of valves were accommodated in unobtrusive housings at running plate level. The compound engine, on the other hand, reverted to the large casings as used on T. W. Worsdell's Class J singles, but as 1619 had an extended smokebox the casings were even larger!

The new engines, particularly the 20 simples, were immediately put to work on East Coast expresses between York and Edinburgh, with a change of engine at Newcastle, and they were nicely run in, with their teething troubles ironed out, in time for the 'Races to Aberdeen' in August 1895. It is known that on the night of 19/20 August 1624 hauled the 'racing' train from York to Newcastle, and 1621 from Newcastle to Edinburgh, and it was on this occasion that the train was extremely fortunate to pass safely round the reverse curves at Portobello at 82mph, especially when there was a speed restriction of 20mph (*vide* NER *Working Timetable Appendix*). It was on this trip that the train was timed by a party of eminent railway enthusiasts and the full story of their exploits is well worth reading in O. S. Nock's book *The Railway Races to the North.* What a pity they were not aboard the final run two nights later when, according to the guard's journal, a time of 113min was recorded for the 124 miles from Newcastle to Edinburgh. On this last run the engine was 1620, which had taken over from 1621 at Newcastle.

The time was not bettered for many years, and even in 1935, when A4 *Silver King* worked a demonstration run from Newcastle to Edinburgh and back, it took 114min in the up direction. The timing for the streamlined 'Coronation' train introduced in 1937 was 120min in each direction.

When new most of the Class M1 engines (probably 15) were stationed at Gateshead, with three at Tweedmouth and two at York. The Gateshead engines worked both north and south from Newcastle and the Geordies were very proud of their magnificent engines. Much of their time was spent on the more difficult north main line north of Newcastle and two or three were usually to be found outstationed at the North British St Margarets shed at Edinburgh, where the North Eastern maintained a small stud of passenger engines. However, the main line traffic was very seasonal and the engines appear to have changed frequently. In fact, with all the unbalanced, light engine, and pilot workings between Newcastle, Tweedmouth and Edinburgh, it makes one wonder why the North Eastern bothered to fight for the right to work the East Coast trains north of Berwick. No doubt prestige was largely responsible.

But fight they did when in 1894 the North British intimated that they wished to work the East Coast trains between Edinburgh and Berwick. Thus it became necessary to station a number of top-link engines at Tweedmouth to re-engine East Coast expresses and by 1898 Tweedmouth shed accommodated 14 Class M1 engines.

As larger engines appeared these engines were displaced to less arduous tasks, such as Newcastle-

Top: Class M1. The first engine of this class appeared in December 1892, being to a straightforward design by Wilson Worsdell. However, the 26in dia cylinders meant that the steamchests for the slide valves had to be placed outside the frames. The tool boxes, placed longitudinally on 1619, were across the tender front on this engine. / *Author's collection*

Above: Class M1. Fortunately in the 1890s someone in Edinburgh had a liking for North Eastern engines and they were photographed at Waverley station and St Margarets shed. This view shows 1626 in original condition, standing at the east end of Waverley. / *LPC*

Carlisle, and Newcastle-Leeds, and Hull acquired a stud for working to Doncaster, Leeds, York and Scarborough. However, some engines remained north of Newcastle, and Tweedmouth and Alnmouth had some for local workings; on occasions the Tweedmouth engines were called upon to assist or replace failed or struggling Atlantics and Pacifics on main line expresses.

One engine, 1628, was withdrawn after the Hull collision in 1927, but normal withdrawal did not commence until October 1931, when 1635 was scrapped. Withdrawal progressed steadily through the 1930s but came to a standstill after the disappearance of 1636 in October 1938 and 1624 in the following month, leaving two engines in traffic, 1621 and 1629. These both managed to survive for some years because of World War II, 1621 continuing on its local passenger duties between Alnwick, Alnmouth and Newcastle, and 1629 working from Middlesbrough and Newport sheds.

In November 1933 No 1620 was offered to the old Railway Museum at York for preservation, but for some reason the Museum Committee did not respond and the engine was withdrawn from service in February 1934 and cut up. Fortunately when 1621 was withdrawn in 1945 it was earmarked for the Museum, and after being carefully renovated at Darlington Works it was ready to take its place in the Museum when it was re-opened on 18 July 1947 after its wartime closure. In November 1974 1621 was moved across to the new National Railway Museum and in the following year it went to the Carriage Works to be repainted, returning to the Museum in time for the opening by the Duke of Edinburgh on 27 September 1975. Since then 1621 has been on display in the Museum, except for four days at York station to take its place in the centenary celebrations in June 1977. If you do visit the Museum look at the marvellous finish achieved by the Carriage Works painters.

Until June 1914 No 1619 was Class M and 1620-39 were Class M1, but when it was decided to drop the figure 1 suffix 1619 was reclassified 3CC and 1620-39 became Class M. When the LNER took over in 1923 the class letter continued to be painted on the front buffer-beam until 1932, when it was changed to D17, the LNER classification. The correct LNER class was actually D17 Part 1 to distinguish these engines from Class Q, which became LNER D17 Part 2. It was originally intended to classify the M engines as LNER D16, but as this was required for the Great Eastern 'Super Clauds' the D17 classification had to be shared by the North Eastern M and Q engines.

For some time after assuming the position of Locomotive Superintendent Wilson Worsdell continued to use his brother's style of livery for new locomotives, which included a claret (or crimson) surround to the splashers and cab. After being in office for three years he devised a new livery, without the claret panels, but it is not clear on which engine this first appeared; however, it could have been on 1622 of Class M for in Henry Tennant's papers there are details of 1622, which was painted in 'the new style' at a cost of £27 6s 6d, compared with the cost of painting a Class J single 'in the old style' of £34 6s 6d, giving a saving of £7. The saving in crimson paint alone amounted to £4 10s! No 1623 appeared in shop grey for the official photographs to be taken at Jarrow Slake and no doubt this engine, together with 1624-39, appeared in the new livery; however, it is difficult to say in what livery 1620 and 1621 first appeared.

Right: Class M1. No 1639, the last of the class, was fitted with piston valves, but again in the outside position. Note the cylindrical steamchests compared with the rectangular pattern on the slide valve engines. Photographed at Edinburgh on 15 October 1894. / *Author's collection*

Below: Class M1. No 1638, also in original condition, but the tender has been fitted with water pick-up apparatus. Note the air vent pipe behind the tool box; for a time the vent pipes were uncovered but a 'bonnet' was later fitted to prevent coal falling down the pipe and into the tank as the tender was being coaled. This view was taken at York. / *LPC*

Above: Class M1. When these engines were rebuilt with piston valves in the more usual position below the smokebox they also lost their extended smokeboxes, which had been fitted originally so that they could more easily be converted to compounds if required. No 1631 was rebuilt in February 1904.
/ Author's collection

Left: Class M1. No 1620, the pioneer engine, leaves York on a down express. This is the engine that ran from Newcastle to Edinburgh in 113min in the 1895 'Races to Aberdeen'.
/ Author's collection

Below: Class M1. When superheaters were fitted, extended smokeboxes had to be refitted to accommodate the superheater header, and this is 1620 in 1925, prepared for running in the Centenary Procession held on 2 July to mark the 100th anniversary of the first Stockton & Darlington train. The livery is LNER green, with the number on the tender. */ Author's collection*

LNER green livery was carried after the Grouping, until in 1928 economy measures brought a change to lined black. At first L N E R (in 7½in transfers) and the engine number (in 12in transfers) appeared on the tender sides, but from 1929 only L N E R (in 12in transfers) appeared on the tender, with the number in the same size on the engine splashers. The number was also carried on the front buffer-beam, with 'No' on the left-hand side of the drawhook and the engine number on the right. Below, in small characters, Class was on the left and the actual class letter on the right facing the engine.

Class M1 Built at Gateshead

Engine	*Built*	*Rebuilt with inside valves*	*Superheated*	*Withdrawn*	*Last Shed*
1620	12/92	5/07	10/17	2/34	Bridlington
1621	3/93	8/05	4/14	7/45	Alnmouth
1622	4/93	6/08	8/15	3/35	Bridlington
1623	5/93	10/03	6/15	5/32	Botanic Gardens
1624	6/93	2/06	11/29	11/38	Alnmouth
1625	6/93	8/06	1/16	10/32	Alnmouth
1626	6/93	4/04	2/15	5/34	Bridlington
1627	6/93	12/07	6/20	12/33	Alnmouth
1628	6/93	11/06	6/15	11/27	Bridlington
1629	6/93	12/08	6/16	9/45	Newport
1630	6/93	7/08	11/16	12/33	Bridlington
1631	6/93	2/04	1/29	7/34	Selby
1632	9/93	4/04	9/20	11/37	Bridlington
1633	9/93	9/08	3/14	11/34	Bridlington
1634	10/93	7/04	8/29	1/35	Bridlington
1635	10/93	3/08	8/19	10/31	Bridlington
1636	11/93	5/07	8/20	10/38	Alnmouth
1637	11/93	9/04	3/21	1/35	Selby
1638	12/93	12/05	5/24	11/37	Bridlington
1639	3/94	4/07	6/14	3/34	Bridlington

Under the LNER 1943 renumbering scheme 1621 was allocated 2108 and 1629 was allocated 2109, but neither engine ran long enough to receive its new number.

Below: Class M1. No 1620 in its final condition: black livery with the number on the splashers, photographed at York in the early 1930s. / *W. L. Good*

Top: Class M1. No 1637 on a heavy East Coast express — the down 'Flying Scotsman' — near Drem after replacing a failed North Eastern Atlantic in 1924. / *C. J. L. Romanes*

Above: Class M1. No 1630 at Kings Cross shed after working through from the North Eastern Area on 9 August 1924. / *Author's collection*

Top right: Class M1. No 1621 at Tweedmouth on a 2-coach local train in the 1930s. This is the engine which worked the record-breaking train from York to Newcastle on the last night of the 1895 'Races'. It is now preserved in the National Railway Museum at York, restored to its North Eastern green livery. / *C. J. L. Romanes*

Centre right: Class M1. A regular duty for Alnmouth engines in the 1930s was to work the 5.40pm empty stock for the Bristol mail train from its daily storage point at Low Fell to Newcastle Central, prior to its departure at 7.10pm. This is 1621 about to depart from the siding at Low Fell. / *Dr P. Ransome-Wallis*

Right: Class M1. In 1941 No 1621's tender was required for use on a new J39 engine, and in replacement it received a smaller tender formerly behind J25 No 2066. This was lettered NE in the wartime style and this new combination was photographed in the Paint Shop yard at Darlington Works. / *British Rail*

L N E R
1621

1621
1621
L N E R

1621
N E

NORTH
EASTERN
1621

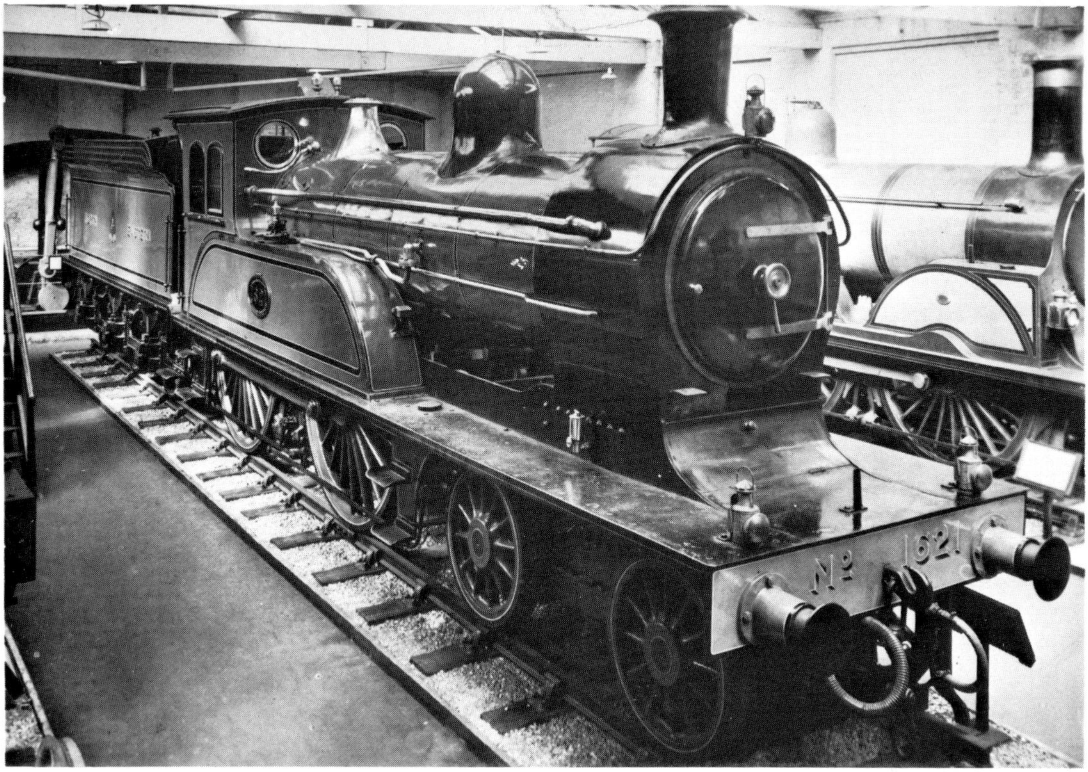
№ 1621

Left: Class M1. No 1621 was withdrawn from Alnmouth shed on 28 July 1945 and subsequently restored to North Eastern livery in readiness for forming one of the exhibits in the Queen Street Railway Museum at York when it reopened in 1947. The engine retained its superheated boiler but regained the correct type of tender. / *British Rail*

Below left: Class M1. No 1621 in Queen Street Museum at York, with *Gladstone* in the background. / *Author's collection*

Top right: Class M1. A top view of 1621's present tender showing the large tank and the exhaust steam 'chimney'. The tank filler lid has been left off. Note the air vent pipes have been removed and the holes blanked off. / *Author's collection*

Centre right: Class M1. No 1621, resplendent in a new coat of paint applied at the Carriage Works, now stands in the National Railway Museum, where it is seen with the author.
/ *Dr A. J. Lowe*

Below: Class M1. Bridlington shed housed a fleet of these engines in LNER days and this view shows a retirement presentation being made to Driver E. Boyes, with his regular engine, 1626, in the background. He had previously been the driver of 1619 until it was scrapped in 1930.
/ *Author's collection*

11 Class Q – W. Worsdell 4-4-0 Introduced 1896

The Class Q engines, the first of which appeared in June 1896, were very similar in size and design to the M1 engines of 1892-4, but there were some differences. Although both classes used the same boiler shell and the same size tubes (1¾in outside diameter) the M1 boiler had 225 tubes and the Q boiler had 201, giving a heating surface of 1,220 and 1,089sq ft respectively. The fireboxes were the same size at 6ft 0½in long by 3ft 2¾in wide, but a slight difference in depth gave an increased heating surface, making the total for M1 1,220 + 121 = 1,341sq ft, and for the Q class 1,089 + 123 = 1,212sq ft.

The M1 engines had slide valves outside the frames operated by rocking levers, whereas the Q engines had slide valves above the cylinders; in both cases Stephenson link motion was used. Both classes had driving wheels 7ft 1¼in dia but the Q cylinders were ½in larger in diameter at 19½in.

There were two noticeable external differences which greatly altered the appearance of the Q engines; they had clerestory roofs to their cabs and brass caps on their chimneys.

The Q class engines rapidly succeeded the M1 class, particularly north of Newcastle, where the longest and heaviest NER locomotive workings took place on the East Coast expresses. The M1 engines had a spell of only three years when they were the prime engines, and the Q engines followed for only three years, because in 1899 the advent of the larger R class brought the North Eastern into the twentieth century with a fleet of 83 4-4-0s all less than ten-years-old. Although the Class R engines dominated the scene, particularly north of Newcastle, there was still plenty of work for the M1, Q and Q1 (see next chapter) engines on the easier (and shorter) routes to York and Leeds.

After they had been displaced from the main line the Qs found many years of employment on the major branch lines, where lighter express work was within their capabilities, and they put in some excellent work day after day between Scarborough, York and Leeds; Hull and York; Hull and Scarborough; West Hartlepool-Northallerton and Harrogate; and Newcastle and Carlisle.

In 1942, when only seven engines remained in traffic, it was decided to remove the long established clerestory roofs to their cabs when next the engines passed through the works. Nos 1871, 1876 and 1921 were scrapped shortly afterwards and are unlikely to have suffered alteration, but 1873, 1902 and 1905 certainly did receive a plain roof. Because of wartime conditions it has not been possible to ascertain if the engine stationed at Duns (1901) was similarly altered, although it was not withdrawn until June 1945. Two engines, 1873 and 1902, managed to survive long enough to become British Railways' property and they were both withdrawn on the same day, 7 February 1948. In their old age they had pottered around on York shed's lightest jobs — the district engineer's inspection saloon, and passenger trains to Pickering and Normanton.

Below: Class Q. This design was basically similar to Class M1, but inside steamchests were fitted from the start, and the cabs had clerestory roofs. This is 1877 at York about 1900. / *Author's collection*

Above right: Class Q. These engines put in a lot of work on the main line and here is 1875 leaving York on a down East Coast express. The field on the right later accommodated carriage sidings and the locomotive shed yard, and on the left Clifton carriage sidings were constructed. In the 19th century the NER standard signal design incorporated the lamp and spectacle some distance below the arm. / *LPC*

Class Q Built at Gateshead

Engine	*Built*	*Superheated*	*1946 number*	*Withdrawn*	*Last shed*
1871	6/96	2/30	2110*	2/44	Alnmouth
1872	6/96	2/14	—	11/33	West Hartlepool
1873	6/96	10/13	2111†	2/48	York
1874	6/96	10/28	—	10/38	Bridlington
1875	9/96	9/15	—	10/31	Neville Hill
1876	9/96	5/15	—	4/43	Haymarket
1877	10/96	1/16	—	10/38	Alnmouth
1878	11/96	10/20	—	2/34	Scarborough
1879	11/96	7/25	—	8/39	Starbeck
1880	12/96	12/18	—	1/33	West Hartlepool
1901	5/97	8/19	2113*	6/45	Duns
1902	6/97	2/20	2112†	2/48	York
1903	6/97	7/27	—	12/36	Starbeck
1904	5/97	9/15	—	10/38	Bridlington
1905	6/97	2/14	2114*	12/43	Alnmouth
1906	6/97	8/28	—	11/38	Alnmouth
1907	6/97	3/17	—	10/38	Botanic Gardens
1908	6/97	4/23	—	11/38	Starbeck
1909	6/97	10/28	—	11/37	Bridlington
1910	6/97	8/22	—	11/38	Bridlington
1921	6/97	8/22	—	4/43	St Margarets
1922	9/97	10/28	—	10/32	Botanic Gardens
1923	9/97	5/24	—	10/38	Alnmouth
1924	10/97	10/13	—	10/37	Carlisle
1925	10/97	10/19	—	11/38	Bradford (Manningham)
1926	10/97	1/14	—	8/31	Carlisle
1927	11/97	4/14	—	10/32	Starbeck
1928	11/97	3/22	—	5/32	Neville Hill
1929	11/97	6/31	—	11/38	Starbeck
1930	11/97	2/14	—	11/33	West Hartlepool

*Number allocated but not carried

†1873 renumbered 2111 2/46 and 1902 renumbered 2112 1/46

Top: Class Q. Another — and later — view of 1877 at York. Changes include front-facing lamp brackets to suit the new standard headlamps, and tool boxes across the tender front. Large crest on tender. / *LPC*

Above: Class Q No 1876 was for long a Carlisle engine and is seen here standing outside the shed c1920. Superheated, with capuchon chimney. Vacuum and Westinghouse brake pipe swan necks removed and hose connections provided below buffer-beam. / *Author's collection*

Left: Class Q. No 1877 has its piston valve cylinders rebored at Neville Hill shed. / *Author's collection*

Below: Class Q. Occasionally North Eastern engines worked through to Kings Cross and this is 1875, probably at Hornsey, in June 1900. / *LPC*

Bottom: Class Q. During a shortage of engines on the Great Eastern section of the LNER in the 1920s a number of North Eastern Area engines went on loan, including No 1927, still in North Eastern livery although in a disreputable state. / *Author's collection*

1871
L N E R

No 1908

Left: Class Q. In the winter of 1939/40 No 1871 was photographed at Darlington after black-out sheets had been fitted between engine and tender, and with gas detector paint on the lower edges of the spectacle glasses. / *British Rail*

Centre left: Class Q. No 1923 leaving Scarborough in 1925. / *Author's collection*

Bottom left: Class Q. No 1908, a Leeds engine, leaves York and passes Holgate excursion platforms, normally used for race traffic. The engine is in LNER green livery. / *Author's collection*

Below: Class Q. No 1905, another Leeds engine at that time, is also passing Holgate platforms but photographed from the up side. The engine is in lined black livery. / *Author's collection*

Bottom: Class Q. Engines of the Q class were also used on the Leeds Northern line, to Harrogate, Northallerton, Stockton and West Hartlepool. This is No 1930, a West Hartlepool engine, leaving Eaglescliffe on 18 May 1923, still in North Eastern livery. / *W. Rogerson*

Above right: Class Q. Another Leeds engine, No 1923, blasts through Headingley on a northbound express. / *Author's collection*

Centre right: Class Q. These engines were also common on the cross-country Newcastle-Carlisle line well into LNER days, and the Carlisle engines were also used to work empty trains into Carlisle Citadel station. This is 1921 standing in one of the bays at the south end of Citadel station. / *Author's collection*

Below: Class Q. Early in LNER days the former North Eastern shed at Carlisle was transferred to Southern Scottish Area control, and eventually the engines were transferred to the former North British shed at Canal, where 1921 was photographed in the 1930s. / *W. L. Good*

Above left: Class Q. The Hull-Scarborough line also saw Class Q engines working from the sheds at both ends of the line, and later from Bridlington. No 1906 of Scarborough was one of the regular engines, seen here leaving Hull (Paragon) on a slow train. / *Author's collection*

Centre left: Class Q. Superheating of Class Q was not completed until June 1931 and this is the last engine to be converted, No 1929, on Dalton Bank, on the main line south of Darlington, on a horsebox and van special on 11 August 1927. At the time 1929 was a Gateshead engine. / *W. Rogerson*

Below: Class Q. Two engines of Class Q survived to become BR property in 1948 — 2111 (ex-1873) and 2112 (ex-1902); during World War II both had lost the clerestory roof to their cabs and 1902 had its tender replaced by a J21 type tender. / *Author's collection*

12 Class Q1 – W. Worsdell 4-4-0 Introduced 1896

The two Q1 engines actually preceded the inaugural batch of Class Q but only by a matter of a few weeks, the reason being that they were intended to counter West Coast competition if 'racing' should be re-introduced in 1896. In the event this did not take place. The Q1 engines were notable in having 7ft 7¼in driving wheels — the largest coupled wheels in the world — but the 4ft 4in diameter boiler was retained, although in this case a 3in longer firebox was fitted compared with the M1 and Q engines. The tube arrangement was the same as on Class Q (201 1¾in od tubes with a length of 11ft 10⅛in) giving a total heating surface of 1,216sq ft.

Another ½in was added to the cylinder diameter, making them 20in compared with the 19½in of Class Q and 19in of Class M1, although 1869 eventually received 19in cylinders in a step towards standardisation of M1, Q and Q1. The longer firebox was also abolished on these two engines and they received a 6ft 9in outside length box instead of the 7ft box originally fitted. No 1869 was superheated in March 1920 but 1870 had been altered five years earlier, in March 1915. Both were withdrawn in October 1930 from Neville Hill shed.

Class Q1 Built at Gateshead

Engine	*Built*	*Superheated*	*Withdrawn*	*Last Shed*
1869	5/96	3/20	10/30	Neville Hill
1870	6/96	3/15	10/30	Neville Hill

Below: Class Q1. These two engines, 1869 and 1870, were famous for having the largest coupled wheels in the world at 7ft 7¼in diameter. The engines were specially designed for working fast trains on the North Eastern section of the East Coast main line, but 'racing' ceased in 1895 and they were used on normal expresses. They had the clerestory roof of the contemporary Class Q engines. / *Author's collection*

Above right: Class Q1. No 1870 at York, with a small shelter for taking indicator diagrams. For a short period at the end of the 19th century the engine number was applied above the drawhook. Note the external communication cord passing through the two eyelets on the tender. / *LPC*

Below right: Class Q1. No 1870 in LNER days, in green livery, with superheating equipment, photographed at York. / *W. L. Good*

1870

L N E R
1870

13 Class R – W. Worsdell 4-4-0 Introduced 1899

The Class R engines, introduced in 1899, were the most successful 4-4-0s ever produced for the North Eastern Railway. From the start they were fitted with outside admission piston valves below the cylinders, although consideration was given to a slide valve version, which would have been Class R1. The boiler was 4ft 9in diameter, 3in larger than on the F and F1 engines, 5in larger than on the M1, Q and Q1 engines, and 3in larger than on the sole example of Class M (1619). The 19in x 26in cylinders were the same size as those on the 20 Class M1 engines, but the driving wheels were of an unusual size for the North Eastern, namely 6ft 10in. The bogie wheels were unusually large at 4ft 0in diameter. With the larger boiler the heating surface was greater than on earlier classes, and even the boiler pressure was raised to 200lb/in^2.

This, then, was a straightforward engine of increased size, eminently suitable for working the East Coast traffic between York and Edinburgh, although it must be conceded that it was about this period that the rapid increase in weight of East Coast trains (with the introduction of coaches weighing 37 to 40 tons) soon put a strain on the Class R engines and the main East Coast expresses had to be handled by 4-6-0 engines until the appearance of the first North Eastern Atlantics in 1903. However, the Class R engines took a large part in East Coast workings right through to the introduction of the Gresley Pacifics in the 1920s. Even then they continued to take their place on secondary workings for another ten years as it was not until the 1930s that they were generally relegated to minor branch line workings.

Details of the very successful and economical working of the first engine, 2011, during the first months of its existence have appeared a number of times, but it is now impossible to tell if this occurred in ordinary day to day running, with routine maintenance, or if it was a specially arranged programme designed to publicise the superiority of the new class*. Publicity or not the engines did perform well so that in 1907, when a larger engine may well have been considered necessary, it was decided to perpetuate the 1899 design and 30 further Class R engines were built. By that time the ten Class V Atlantics had been running for four years and it says something for the efficiency of the 4-4-0s that their

**The Locomotive Railway Carriage & Wagon Review* Vol XXVI p240 and Vol LV p153

Below: Class R. No 2015 was chosen for the official photograph of the class, in grey livery and with the new version of the company's crest on the tender. Tender fitted with water pick up gear with square dome and small vent pipes. / *British Rail*

Above: Class R. The pioneer engine, 2011, at York c1903. / *LPC*

numbers were doubled rather than build further Atlantics. After all, the Atlantics could only be spread very thinly over the system when the North Eastern was responsible for all the East Coast trains over the 205 miles of line between York and Edinburgh.

Apart from the fitting of superheated boilers to all 60 engines between October 1912 and April 1929 few major alterations were made during the 58 years the class worked on the North Eastern and its successors. Some of the engines were fitted with deeper frames, commencing with 2027 in 1911, but this was not, as might have been expected, to take a superheated boiler as 2027 emerged from North Road Works still in its original saturated form, although it did receive a superheated boiler when it next visited North Road two years later.

In LNER days four engines were rebuilt with inside admission piston valves above the cylinders, with the travel of the valves increased from $4^{11}/_{32}$in to 6in. The first to be rebuilt, No 2020, underwent various external modifications including a running plate raised to clear the coupling rods, narrow splashers to the driving wheels, an all-steel cab, and alterations to the tender, but the only noticeable difference on the other three, Nos 592, 2101 and 62375, was the change from right-hand to left-hand drive; their running plates, splashers, cabs and tenders were unaltered.

These four engines took their turn with the unrebuilt engines, although in 1937 No 2020 was usually reserved for working the 'Yorkshire Pullman' from Harrogate to Doncaster via York. However, a most noticeable feature of the rebuilt engines was the sharpness of their exhaust, and John Mallon recalls that when returning light engine from Alnwick to Alnmouth, after working the 5.07pm from Newcastle, the drivers used to open the regulator fully to blast out some of the fire, so that the firemen had less to throw out when stabling the engine at Alnmouth shed. When this occurred the exhaust could be heard over a large area, and over a greater area if the engine happened to be one of Alnmouth's D20/2 engines!

In May 1929 No 2014 of Hull was fitted with a modified blastpipe and chimney, and tried out working from Starbeck shed on the 'Yorkshire Pullman' as far as Doncaster. More than a year later, actually in August 1940, the engine was transferred from Hull to Starbeck in exchange for 2101, the reason given being that 2014 was required at Starbeck for tests! However, it is not clear from the Locomotive Running Superintendent's records if this referred to further tests, or if it was a transfer which took more than a year to pass through the official channels before being recorded.

A description of the lines over which the D20 engines operated would include almost every line in the North East. At first, being the North Eastern's main passenger engines, they were naturally used almost exclusively on the main line between York, Newcastle and Edinburgh, but after the doubling of the former Leeds Northern branch between Northallerton and Melmerby in 1901 they began to work Newcastle-Sunderland-Stockton-Harrogate-Leeds services, usually on the through trains to Liverpool.

As larger engines appeared — the R1 4-4-0s and V

and Z Atlantics — the Class R engines were used on the more important branches, although for some years they still appeared on the main line, often handling unaided trains normally worked by Atlantics. In LNER days their main line duties were usually confined to the semi-fast and stopping passenger trains, but during World War II there was a period when they returned to East Coast expresses, usually in harness with a D49 4-4-0, thus releasing a large engine — usually a V2 2-6-2 — for a freight or troop train.

After World War II the ageing D20s worked branches where they had never been seen before, such as Northallerton-Hawes-Garsdale. Two branches on which they were not normally seen were those from Hull to Hornsea and Withernsea, where the turntables were too small to accommodate them.

Their main spheres of operation in the 1950s, their final years, were from Alnmouth, Bridlington, Northallerton, Selby and Starbeck sheds. In fact 17 of the class were withdrawn from Alnmouth between May 1949 and November 1957; as one of the class was scrapped another was transferred to Alnmouth to take its place — until there were no more replacements! Nos 62381 (1042) and 62396 (1665) were withdrawn from Alnmouth on 19 November 1957 and 62395 (1260) was withdrawn on the following day. In North Eastern days 1042 was reputed to be the best of the class.

Right: Class R. No 2011 at Neville Hill shed c1921, after being fitted with a superheated boiler and extended smokebox. / *Author's collection*

Class R Built at Gateshead

Engine	*Built*	*Superheated*	*1946 number**	*BR number**	*Withdrawn*	*Last shed*
476	9/06	6/15	2370	(62370)	4/51	Starbeck
592	9/06	2/15	2371	62371	10/54	Alnmouth (See Note)
707	10/06	10/17	2372	62372	11/56	Bridlington
708	10/06	1/21	2373	62373	2/53	Northallerton
711	10/06	5/15	2374	62374	10/54	Selby
712	11/06	7/20	2375	62375	5/57	Alnmouth (See Note)
713	11/06	8/15	2376	(62376)	2/51	Selby
723	11/06	2/20	2377	(62377)	5/49	Alnmouth
724	12/06	2/15	2378	62378	11/56	Selby
725	12/06	8/17	2379	62379	4/51	West Hartlepool
1026	2/07	3/14	2380	62380	9/54	Gateshead
1042	3/07	6/19	2381	62381	11/57	Alnmouth
1051	6/07	2/14	2382	(62382)	2/51	Selby
1078	6/07	6/14	2383	62383	5/57	Alnmouth
1147	3/07	1/17	—	—	1/43	West Hartlepool
1184	6/07	6/14	2384	62384	8/55	Selby
1206	4/07	6/17	(2385)	—	1/45	Starbeck
1207	8/07	4/13	2386	62386	10/56	Selby
1209	4/07	10/17	2387	62387	9/57	Alnmouth
1210	8/07	3/14	2388	62388	4/54	Northallerton
1217	5/07	12/14	2389	62389	9/54	Neville Hill
1223	9/07	12/16	2390	(62390)	11/48	Stockton
1232	5/07	3/18	2391	62391	6/51	Northallerton
1234	5/07	4/29	—	—	5/43	Bridlington
1235	9/07	11/13	2392	62392	5/54	Selby
1236	6/07	12/17	2393	—	12/47	Starbeck
1258	9/07	11/17	2394	—	5/46	Starbeck
1260	6/07	11/14	2395	62395	11/57	Alnmouth
1665	9/07	8/20	2396	62396	11/57	Alnmouth
1672	9/07	8/13	2397	62397	2/57	Bridlington
2011	8/99	10/17	2340	62340	2/51	Selby
2012	9/99	5/14	2341	62341	3/51	Selby
2013	9/99	10/12	2342	62342	3/51	Selby

Engine	*Built*	*Superheated*	*1946 number**	*BR number**	*Withdrawn*	*Last shed*
2014	10/99	10/16	2343	62343	10/56	Selby
2015	11/99	1/15	2344	62344	3/51	Alnmouth
2016	11/99	1/16	2345	62345	10/56	Selby
2017	11/99	12/14	(2346)	—	12/44	Scarborough
2018	12/99	9/13	2347	62347	11/54	Northallerton
2019	12/99	10/15	2348	62348	2/51	Selby
2020	12/99	5/14	2349	62349	2/56	Selby (See Note)
2021	8/00	3/15	2350	—	12/47	Selby
2022	8/00	2/13	2351	62351	11/54	Alnmouth
2023	9/00	9/21	2352	62352	6/54	Gateshead
2024	9/00	1/15	2353	62353	4/51	Bridlington
2025	9/00	3/25	2354	62354	4/51	Alnmouth
2026	10/00	11/12	2355	62355	11/55	Alnmouth
2027	10/00	2/14	(2356)	—	11/46	Starbeck
2028	11/00	4/18	2357	62357	1/51	Alnmouth
2029	12/00	5/14	2358	62358	10/54	Alnmouth
2030	12/00	2/18	2359	62359	10/55	Neville Hill
2101	12/00	4/19	2360	62360	10/56	Alnmouth (See Note)
2102	12/00	6/16	2361	(62361)	2/51	Selby
2103	12/00	7/18	2362	62362	4/51	Alnmouth
2104	2/01	8/14	2363	62363	3/51	Selby
2105	3/01	7/15	2364	—	10/47	Starbeck
2106	3/01	2/15	2365	62365	4/51	Alnmouth
2107	3/01	4/15	2366	62366	3/51	Selby
2108	4/01	11/15	2367	(62367)	1/48	Botanic Gardens
2109	4/01	11/12	(2368)	—	6/44	Botanic Gardens
2110	5/01	9/17	2369	62369	3/51	Starbeck

*Engine numbers in brackets in columns 4 and 5 indicate that the number was allocated but was not actually carried

Note

Four engines were rebuilt to Class D20/2 as follows: October 1936 No 2020; October 1942 No 592; January 1943 No 2101; October 1948 No 62375 (ex-712)

Top: Class R. No 2105 'on shed' at York. The fireman has just opened the smokbox door: note the amount of 'char' that has accumulated in the smokebox — up to the level of the blastpipe top. / *Author's collection*

Above: Class R. No 2020 standing at No 5 platform (now No 9) at York, with R1 No 1246 waiting on the through road. The crank and rod from the base of the smokebox on 2020 indicate that this was one of the class fitted with W. Worsdell's variable blastpipe, which was under the control of the driver. / *Author's collection*

Top right: Class R. Twelve of this class were fitted with deeper frames and 2027 was the first to be treated, in July 1911. It was photographed in the Works Yard at Darlington. / *Author's collection*

Centre right: Class R. Preliminary trials with different types of superheater were carried out on 1235, which received an extended smokebox for this reason. It is seen here on a down express at Beningbrough. / *LPC*

Right: Class R. At a later date 2013 also had an extended smokebox, which it retained until 1930. Until 1924 it was a Neville Hill engine, where this photograph was taken. It then moved to Scarborough, where it spent 10 years on workings to York, Leeds and Hull. / *Author's collection*

2027
NORTH EASTERN

Left: Class R. This photograph of 2019 was taken to illustrate the rotary switch (attached to the main frames between the bogie wheels) for the electrical version of Raven's cab signalling apparatus. / *Author's collection*

Below: Class R. The Class R engines retained the LNER green livery until 1929, and some acquired the letter D suffix used in early LNER days to distinguish former North Eastern engines. No 2022D was photographed at York. / *LPC*

Top right: Class R. No 2019 at Darlington in LNER green. / *R. H. Inness*

Centre right: Class R. This official photograph shows 2011 with the number immediately below the cab windows instead of inside the rear brass beading, although traces of the number in its correct position can be seen. It seems probable, from a close inspection of the print, that the number was put in its new position solely by photographic manipulation, and that the engine did not actually carry the number in the position indicated. / *British Rail*

Bottom right: Class R. No 592 actually did carry its number just below the cab windows after the rear semi-circular brass beading had been removed. The engine is shown rebuilt to Class D20/2, with piston valves above the cylinders and converted to left hand drive after modification in 1942. The new frames are a combination of the Worsdell and Raven pattern. / *British Rail*

L N E R
2019

2011
L N E R

592

Top left: Class R. No 1051, a Gateshead engine at the time, at Kings Cross shed in August 1924. This engine has L & N E R on the tender. / *LPC*

Centre left: Class R. No 1147, with bogie removed, receiving attention at Hull Dairycoates in the 1930s. / *T. E. Rounthwaite*

Below: Class R. The first engine to be rebuilt to D20/2 was 2020 in October 1936; unlike the later engines it received a new cab and splashers, and the tender had the backed coal rails replaced by solid sheeting. After a spell at York 2020 went to Starbeck shed in 1937 to work the up 'Yorkshire Pullman' from Harrogate to Doncaster when it was re-routed via York. / *British Rail*

Top right: Class R. No 1223 at work on the Newcastle-Carlisle line near Wylam on 5 June 1920. / *W. Rogerson*

Centre right: Class R. No 723 on an up express at Alnmouth on 2 August 1920. / *W. Rogerson*

Bottom right: Class R. No 2106 leaving York on a 4-coach local composed wholly of NER clerestory stock. The engine is in a hybrid livery with L.N.E.R. and the number on the tender, but it retains its large brass NER numberplate on the splasher. / *H. L. Salmon*

Nº 1223

Nº 723

L N E
9826

Left: Class R. No 1260 on a down express just north of Northallerton station, with the Hawes branch diverging on the right, and the low level Leeds Northern line in the background on the left. / *Author's collection*

Centre left: Class R, No 1210 at Galashiels. / *Author's collection*

Bottom left: Class R. Tweedmouth engines worked Berwick-Edinburgh slow trains and some terminated or commenced at Corstorphine. This is 1210 passing through Princes Street Gardens en route to Waverley and on to Berwick. / *Author's collection*

Below: Class R. A regular summer Saturday working for Selby engines in the 1950s was for a pair of them on the 11.20am Scarborough-Liverpool, seen here leaving Bridlington in August 1954. The engines, 62395 (ex-1260) and 62381 (ex-1042) worked as far as Gascoigne Wood and then returned light to Selby. / *J. W. Armstrong*

Bottom: Class R. In the winter months some D20s, including 62387 (ex-1209), spent their time in store at Scarborough. On this occasion, 28 May 1957, 62387 had been taken out of store and specailly cleaned to work a rail tour a few days later. Here it is outside Scarborough shed, being prepared to work light engine to York. The tender was one of those fitted with a new tank and this was eventually mounted on the frames of a Q6 tender when the latter's tank was badly damaged in a collision. / *Author*

62360
MANCHESTER
HULL
62360

62351

62384
62384

Top left: Class R. The third engine to be rebuilt to D20/2 was 2101 (later 62360) in January 1943, retaining Raven pattern frames. In the 1950s it was used on rail tours, including one of the first — the SLS/MLS special from Manchester to Hull via former Midland and Hull & Barnsley lines in August 1952. It is seen here at Hull Botanic Gardens shed ready for working the return special as far as Cudworth. / *Author*

Centre left: Class R. Brass strip carrying the BR number as attached to the numberplate of 62351 in 1948. Mounted on a polished wooden base it is now used as a paperweight. / *Author*

Left: Class R. Although attempts were made to preserve one of these engines they were unsuccessful and all 60 ended up in the scrapyard at Darlington, including 62384 (ex-1184) in September 1955. / *Author*

Top: Class R. The last of the Class R to be withdrawn was 62395 (ex-1260) on 20 November 1957. Eleven days later it was found standing forlornly in the scrapyard covered in frost! / *Author*

Above: Class R. When preservation of 62395 was refused British Rail, as a concession, decided to paint the engine roughly (in unlined black) on one side only so that an official record of the last engine could be obtained. It was then cut up for scrap. / *British Rail*

14 Class R1 – W. Worsdell 4-4-0 Introduced 1908

The North Eastern 4-4-0 line ended with the R1 engines, which first appeared from Darlington Works in November 1908. The ten engines were numbered 1237-1246 and in appearance they were massive looking engines, with their 5ft 6in dia boilers pitched at 8ft 11in. The typical Worsdell cab was retained, albeit with a pronounced arch to the roof greater than on any of the earlier 4-4-0 designs. Gone, however, were the long splashers covering both coupled wheels, and instead separate splashers were fitted, wide enough to take wheels and coupling rods.

The boiler was similar to, but shorter than, the Class V boiler of 1903, both having 254 2in tubes in the original saturated form. The grate area was the same as on the two-cylinder Atlantics, but the firebox heating surface was less because the depth of the firebox on the R1 engines was restricted by the rear axle.

Compared with the Class R engines the main difference, apart from the enlarged boiler, was the increase in the overhang at the rear end from 4ft 4in to 6ft 5in, giving comparative distances from rear driving axle to leading tender axle of 9ft 9⅞in for Class R and 11ft 8¾in for Class R1. The wheelbase of the two 4-4-0 classes was the same at 23ft 9in, made up of 6ft 6in bogie, 7ft 6in rear bogie wheel to leading driving wheel, and 9ft 6in coupled wheelbase. The R1 engines were fitted with the more usual size of bogie wheels of 3ft 7¼in dia compared with the 4ft 0in wheels on Class R.

Although the R and R1 fireboxes were the same width (3ft 11in outside) to fit between the frames, the R1 firebox was 9ft 0in long compared with the 7ft 0in of the R, giving an increased grate area of 27sq ft compared with 20sq ft. To cover the grate with coal 1ft deep the fireman had to shift 12cwt of coal on an R1 compared with 9cwt on a Class R! No wonder crews preferred the Class R engines and referred to the

R1 engines as 'big b******s', or even 'big useless b*****s', from which it will be gathered that this final North Eastern 4-4-0 design was not entirely popular! Dislike could be even greater if a fireman had not run his fire well down at the end of a journey and some unfortunate shed crew had to throw out the fire a shovelful at a time — no rocking or drop grates then! I have been told that extra-long prickers and fireshovels were provided for the fireboxes of these engines.

Originally the working pressure was 225lb, soon reduced to 180lb. A start on superheating the class was made in August 1912 (No 1244) and all were converted within three years. In fact 1244 was the first North Eastern engine to be converted from saturated to superheated under the conversion programme, although other engines had been converted temporarily during experiments held in the first decade of the century, and ten superheated Atlantics (Class Z1) had been obtained in 1911.

Instead of placing the Westinghouse pump between the wheels and inside the splashers it was mounted on a vertical column on the right-hand side of the smokebox. Screw reverse was standard on the class. Two sets of Ramsbottom safety valves were fitted and the two 'tails' had to curve down to enter the cab just below the roof. Thus the brass trumpet covering the valves had to be fatter and more squat than on the other 4-4-0s; when Ross 'pop' valves were fitted their bases were covered by a polished brass mounting.

Stepping on to the footplate of an R1 engine for the first time gave an immediate impression of their size. The regulator gland was at a height of some 6ft 6in above the fall plate, and the rams-horn regulator extended well above that! The top of the boiler was about 7ft 6in above the fall plate, lost in the gloom at the top of the cab, whilst the girth of the back end of the firebox left little space between the sides of the 7ft 5in wide cab. A wooden cab floor was provided, sloping gently upwards to the front with, of course, the usual wooden footstools on either side. These were an absolute necessity to reach the regulator handle, even for a driver of medium height. The usual metal boxes with wooden seat boards were provided on each side of the cab over the driving wheels. However, the cab side windows suffered from the usual fault of being too low for comfort and convenience.

Below left: Class R1. The final and largest NER design of 4-4-0 appeared in November 1908 but only 10 engines were built. They were massive engines, weighing 105 tons 2cwt in working order, but they were noted coal eaters and they were not liked. This official photograph shows 1238, the second engine to be built, photographed at Darlington, where they were the first large passenger engines to be built. / *British Rail*

Below: Class R1. After more than 20 years' use the long splasher over both coupled wheels was abandoned, and a new position was found for the Westinghouse pump. The two sets of safety valves required a large squat brass cover, as seen on 1242 at Neville Hill. / *Author's collection*

L N E R
1239

N E R
1244

When new these engines were used on the East Coast expresses on the main line, but most of their life was spent on more menial duties; in the 1920s a small stud at Hull was responsible for working Sheffield trains and the Leeds engines were used mainly for working to Hull and Scarborough, with forays north to Newcastle at time of pressure. During the winter months they pottered around on the Leeds Northern line from Leeds to Harrogate, Northallerton, Stockton and West Hartlepool, with a load of a few ex-North Eastern bogie coaches. One of the Starbeck engines was at one time responsible for a working from Harrogate to Doncaster, reversing at Leeds Central and working a GN section train from Leeds to Doncaster via Wakefield: this engine returned on the Harrogate portion of the 1.40pm from Kings Cross, running via Knottingley, Church Fenton and Tadcaster, succeeding the Great Northern engine once stationed at Starbeck for this duty. In 1926 No 1237 was even seen on the down 'Harrogate Pullman', which it worked from Harrogate to Newcastle, although this was probably to replace a Heaton engine which had been unable to take up its return working.

On 4 August 1910, only nine weeks after being appointed Chief Mechanical Engineer, Raven put before the Locomotive Committee a request for permission to order 12 'express passenger engines based on Class R1'. Somewhere along the line it was decided that these engines would have the 4-4-2 wheel arrangement and thus when the tenders were opened on 27 October 1910 they were for three-cylinder Atlantic engines; it was decided to increase the order to 20 and to place the contract with the North British Locomotive Co Ltd of Glasgow. However, that some consideration was given to an improved R1 design is borne out by an undated Gateshead drawing for a three-cylinder 4-4-0; fortunately it has been annotated 'R.10 Prop' indicating that it was a proposal initiated in 1910 for a modified 4-4-0.

This outline drawing depicts an engine identical with Class R1 except that it had three cylinders 17in x 26in in place of the two 19in x 26in of the 1908 engines. The estimated weight on the bogie was 18 tons, 10cwt heavier than on the R1 engines, making the total estimated weight of engine and tender in working order 105 tons 12cwt, but all the other dimensions — boiler diameter, tube heating surface, grate area, tender capacity etc — were unchanged.

The progression from proposed three cylinder 4-4-0 to Class Z Atlantic was relatively easy and basically, probably over-simplifying the matter, the Atlantic was a 'stretched' version of the 4-4-0, with a similar but longer boiler, and a similar but deeper firebox:

	Proposed 4-4-0	*Class Z*
Rear bogie to leading driver	7ft 9in	7ft 5in
Coupled wheelbase	9ft 6in	7ft 7in
Diameter of boiler	5ft 6in	5ft 6in
Length of boiler	11ft 6in	15ft 10½in
Length of firebox	9ft 0in	9ft 0in
Firebox heating surface	158sq ft*	180sq ft
Grate area	27sq ft	27sq ft
Tubes — number and diameter	254 x 2in	254 x 2in
Pitch of boiler	8ft 11in	8ft 11in

*Depth of firebox on 4-4-0 restricted by rear axle

On the Class Z (saturated) Atlantics the cylinders were 15½in x 26in, and on the Z1 (superheated) engines 16½in x 26in.

Above left: Class R1. No 1239 at York after working the Newcastle 'diner' from Hull on 10 May 1927. The engine has been fitted with a superheated boiler but retains the original safety valves. / *H. G. W. Household*

Left: Class R1. No 1244 from the rear, standing outside Scarborough shed in June 1939. / *W. B. Greenfield*

Class R1 Built at Darlington

Engine	*Built*	*Superheated*	*GN tender*	*1946 number*	*Withdrawn*	*Last shed*
1237	11/08	7/15	7/41	2217*	3/45	Neville Hill
1238	12/08	12/12	6/41	2218*	3/45	Neville Hill
1239	12/08	6/14	5/41	—	12/42	Neville Hill
1240	3/09	4/15	5/41	2219*	5/44	Neville Hill
1241	6/09	7/15	7/41	—	3/43	Starbeck
1242	6/09	9/12	8/41	2220*	1/46	Neville Hill
1243	6/09	1/13	5/41	2221*	6/45	Neville Hill
1244	7/09	8/12	6/41	2222*	10/44	Neville Hill
1245	8/09	7/15	8/41	2223*	2/46	Neville Hill
1246	8/09	3/13	5/41	2224*	7/43	Starbeck

*Number allocated but not carried

Top: No 1237 on the down 'Scotsman' picking up water at Wiske Moor troughs, with the NER dynamometer car as the first vehicle, followed by the Normanton-Edinburgh mail van, probably taken in February 1909. / *LPC*

Above: Class R1. No 1240 enters York on the morning Leeds-Glasgow train, subsequently known as the 'North Briton'. / *S. Ellingworth*

Top right: Class R1. No 1239 leaving York, photographed from Holgate platforms. / *LPC*

Centre right: Class R1. No 1241 on a down express on the main line near Eryholme on 8 June 1930. / *W. Rogerson*

Right: Class R1. No 1243 leaving York on a Leeds train. / *C. Ord*

No 1239

176

Top: Class R1. Another of the R1 class on the main line at Eryholme — this time 1240 on 5 August 1933. / *W. Rogerson*

Above: Class R1. To release their tenders for new J39 engines the R1 class received redundant ex-Great Northern tenders and an official photograph was taken of 1246 with the tender off 4-4-0 No 4378. / *British Rail*

Right: Class R1. In November 1941 a Hull-Scarborough train was attacked by a German aircraft between Bridlington and Filey. The aircraft flew low over the train and when a bomb was dropped it was travelling almost horizontally, so that when it hit the tender it passed out of the back and did not explode! The engine was 1242, then running with the tender from ex-Great Northern 4-4-0 No 4348. / *British Rail*

15 Tenders

All the tenders built for the Worsdell 4-4-0s were on an equally divided 12ft 8in wheelbase, with a water capacity of 3,038 to 4,125 gallons depending on the size of the engine. The coal capacity was normally 5 tons but it was 5½ tons on Class R1. At first two coal rails ran along each side of the tender and across the back, but when these were increased to three, a fourth rail was added along each side but not reaching to the back of the tender. The four-rail section along each side had a backing plate to prevent small coal falling through, and a plate across the tender, joining the ends of the four-rail section, separated the coal space from the tank filler.

The two Q1 engines, 1869 and 1870, were the first to be fitted with water scoops when they were built in 1896; these were for use at the water troughs at Lucker, between Newcastle and Edinburgh, followed a few years later by the troughs at Wiske Moor, near Northallerton. The tenders of the earlier M1 and Q engines were subsequently fitted with scoops and the R and R1 engines were built with them. The water scoop screw handle was on the left-hand side of the tender, with a similar handle for the handbrake on the right-hand side.

In North Eastern days the engine number was shown at the rear of the tender, on the curved panel at the top, but as the standard LNER livery included the engine number in large characters on each side of the tender, below the initials of the new company, no indication of the number was considered necessary on the back.

However, with the 1929 decision to carry the number on the engine, leaving only the initials on the sides of the tender, some form of tender identification became necessary and it was decided to fit a cast oval plate (giving the engine number and building details) on the rear panel of the tender.

Although 'tender swapping' was not encouraged it was sometimes carried out at running sheds when an engine was stopped for repairs; its serviceable tender could then be used behind an engine of the same class which had its own tender under repair. This led to the appearance in 1926 of engine 2024 with tender 723.

In 1938 the North Eastern Area of the LNER decided to renumber its stock of tenders in a series commencing at 7001. This was influenced by the fact that an engine took longer to repair than a tender and consequently a tender was often standing in the yard at the works awaiting its locomotive. It was, therefore, more economical for an engine to take a suitable tender from a float of repaired tenders, and henceforward the exchange of tenders became more prevalent.

Under the 1938 scheme the tender numbers allocated were:

Class	*Engines in stock*	*Tender numbers*
D17/1	4	8584-7
D17/2	18	8588-8605
D20	60	8371-8430
D21	10	8686-95

Some tenders from 4-4-0s were used after withdrawal to replace worn out tenders behind other engines. A few examples:

Tender from	*Class*	*To*	*Class*
42	D22	22	J21
521	D23	1120	D23
1539	D22	1723	J25
1545	D22	470	J21
1619	D19	1905	D17/2

Other tenders were used for water carriers, such as those from D17/2 1923; D18 1869; D22 194, 514, 684, 1532; D23 214, 1107.

In 1949 10 D20 tenders were fitted with new tanks with straight sides, leading to the suggestion that these were LNER standard tenders transferred from some other class, possibly J39. This was not so — they were simply new tanks on the original frames, and the tenders retained their 1938 numbers. Altogether these ten tenders ran at various times behind 14 D20s: 62341/3/8/51/3/5/ 8/74/80/1/3/6/7/97. Although no D20 ran with more than one rebuilt tender, four tenders ran behind two different D20s: tender 8381 ran behind 62380 and 62383; tender 8402 behind 62353 and 62374; tender 8416 behind 62355 and

62343; tender 8941 behind 62386 and 62387. The other six tenders were numbered 8384, 8409/12/3/8/9.

About September 1957 Q6 0-8-0 63400 was involved in a collision at Pelaw and its tender tank was badly damaged. When 63400 was in Darlington Works for repairs, D20 No 62387 arrived for scrapping and as the tank on 62387's tender was in good condition it was decided to transfer it on to the frame and wheels of 63400's tender. The number-plate on the rear of the tender was changed from 8941 to 8742 — the Q6's correct tender number — and this modified tender continued to run behind 63400 and other Q6 engines until it was sold for scrap in August 1966.

On his Class I and J 'singles' T. W. Worsdell introduced a simple form of feedwater heating, whereby some of the exhaust steam could be turned into the water in the tank on the tender, and this system was perpetuated by his brother on the M1 4-4-0 engines. Surplus steam was allowed to escape through a conical casting, mounted at the top of a large diameter pipe towards the back of the tender on some engines; but on others, fitted with larger tanks extending above the two coal rails, the casting was bolted directly on to the top of the tank.

It is said that when running, engines with this apparatus left two trails of steam, one from the engine chimney and one from the tender vent. One of the tenders with the large pattern tanks, with the exhaust casting on top, can be seen on 1621 in the National Railway Museum at York, admirably placed for viewing from the gallery.

When tenders were required for the new J39 0-6-0 engines built at Darlington in 1941 it was decided to use the tenders from the D21 engines, and to replace them with redundant Great Northern tenders. Thus the following changes took place:

D21 engine	*Tender to J39*	*Replaced on D21 by GN tender from*
1237	3096	4345 4-4-0
1238	3093	267 4-2-2
1239	3090	4376 4-4-0
1240	3088	4332 4-4-0
1241	3095	4384 4-4-0
1242	3098	4348 4-4-0
1243	3091	4329 4-4-0
1244	3094	3278 4-4-2
1245	3097	4324 4-4-0
1246	3092	4378 4-4-0

The use of these ex-Great Northern tenders meant that the Westinghouse brake had to be removed from the D21 engines and they were converted to vacuum brake.

16 Accidents Involving 4-4-0s

With a working life spread over 70 years it is only to be expected that some of the McDonnell and Worsdell 4-4-0s would be involved in accidents and it is unfortunate that a number of these proved to be major incidents, with loss of life.

The first occurred at Ryhope, on the line from Stockton to Sunderland, on 19 August 1889. At that time there was no direct route along the coast from Stockton, through West Hartlepool, to Sunderland and trains had to turn inland and travel via Thorpe Thewles, Wellfield and Murton before descending Seaton Bank to Ryhope. Seaton Bank was originally a rope-worked incline on the Durham & Sunderland Railway opened in 1836, but about 1860 it was converted to a locomotive line. From Murton the falling gradients were:

1 mile 26 chains at 1 in	205
9 chains at 1 in	88.5
14 chains at 1 in	39
1 mile 14 chains at 1 in	44
24 chains at 1 in	48.4
55 chains at 1 in	60

Thus there were 3¾ miles of which 2¼ miles were at between 1 in 60 and 1 in 39.

The train was the 2pm from Liverpool to Newcastle and as it was running some 16min late the driver entered the steepest part of the bank at 40mph or more, expecting that his Westinghouse brake would bring the speed down far enough to negotiate safely the 11½ chain curve immediately beyond Ryhope station.

However, the brake had not enough effect, even though sand was applied to the rails, and the train entered the curve at 30mph or more, where it was considered 15mph was the highest safe speed, although no instruction was issued to that effect by the NER. Consequently the engine and six of the seven coaches were derailed and finished on their sides on the outside of the curve. The engine, F1 No 663 (at the time of the accident less than two-years-old) was severely damaged but it was repaired and put back into traffic. It was worked by a Gateshead crew, which had earlier worked south (as far as Leeds) on the 10am Newcastle-Liverpool via the same route.

This accident led to the issue of an instruction that every passenger train descending the bank must come to a momentary halt in Ryhope station, thus ensuring that the driver retained control during the descent of Seaton Bank and could only traverse the curve at a low speed after starting from rest at Ryhope. The instruction appears to have remained in force for 70 years but it lapsed in 1960.

A most serious accident occurred at Castle Hills, just north of Northallerton, on 4 October 1894, not far from the site of the notable Manor House collision of 1892. The two accidents were similar in that an up night express crashed into the rear of a mineral train, although the causes were completely different. In this collision M1 1622 was attached to the 10.40pm Edinburgh-Kings Cross at Newcastle and, after having difficulty with his Westinghouse brake pump, and as the engine was not steaming very well, the driver decided to take a pilot from Darlington to help him reach York and the train left Darlington at 2.40am, 12min late, with 2-4-0 No 905 as pilot.

The driver of the leading engine (who was killed) ran past signals at danger, whilst the driver of 1622 missed seeing all the distant and home signals at three locations because of fog, and steam from the leading engine, relying on the driver of 905 to take any necessary action. Consequently the express collided with the rear of the 1.40am mineral train from Darlington to York, which was about to be shunted into a siding to allow the express to pass.

Although the results of the collision were spectacular, with a large amount of wreckage spread over the tracks, no passengers were killed, although 19 were injured. The train engine (1622) and crew were from York shed.

The two engines were repaired and restored to traffic and 1622, then a comparatively new engine, continued to run until 1935.

In 1894 the North British Railway was challenging the North Eastern's right to work all East Coast trains between Berwick and Edinburgh, and until the dispute was settled engines were changed at Berwick. On 31 July 1897 Q1 No 1869 worked a northbound train from Newcastle to Berwick and stood there from 6.40am to 1.53pm before taking over the 12.20pm Edinburgh to Kings Cross, which left Berwick for Newcastle 24min late. The driver did not need to use his brake until approaching Newcastle and by then it was too late to do anything when he found it was having no effect, and the train ran into Central station at about 20mph. Standing in the platform was a 10-coach train from Tynemouth, from which the engine had just been uncoupled, and ahead of that six empty coaches, and 1869 hit the rear of the Tynemouth train at 10 to 15mph.

It transpired that the fireman on 1869 had omitted to open one of the brake pipe cocks when coupling up at Berwick: the driver had not bothered to check that the coupling up was performed correctly, and the guard omitted to carry out a brake test! The engine was badly damaged and damage to the stationary coaches was extensive.

One of the luckiest escapes of a North Eastern train occurred at Darlington in the early hours of 16 April 1904. Again it was an East Coast express that was involved, this time the 8.15pm from Kings Cross, which was taken over at York by R No 2025 and Q No 1923. The train was not booked to call at Darlington and consequently was routed to pass outside the station, when it collided with Class E 0-6-0T No 263 standing on the down main and overlooked by the signalman. The crew of the shunting engine saw the express approaching and, after the driver had opened the regulator to set the engine off in the same direction as the rapidly approaching express, they abandoned their footplate as quickly as they could and left the luckless 263 to its fate!

When the express caught up with No 263 the front end of the leading engine (2025) forced its way under the back end of the tank engine and pushed it forward some 320yd; fortunately the leading wheels of the 0-6-0T kept the rails! At the same time the front end of the second engine (1923) went under the rear end of the tender of 2025 and the three engines went along locked together until the express stopped. No damage was caused to the coaches and the train continued its journey with a fresh engine.

The driver of 2025 was George Turner, who had driven 1621 on the night of 21/22 August 1895 during the 'Races to Aberdeen'.

On the night of 1 November 1906 some wagons of a Glasgow-London braked goods were derailed between East Fortune and East Linton, on the North British section of the East Coast main line, fouling the down track. The driver of the goods rapidly appreciated the situation and, knowing that the down express was due, he quickly uncoupled his engine and started forward, with his fireman going along the running plate to show two red lights instead of two white lights. The driver also sounded a warning whistle so that the North Eastern driver, Alex Davidson, with his regular Class R No 592 on the 2,20pm from Kings Cross, was able to apply his brakes, put on his steam sands, and reverse his engine before hitting the derailed wagons. Fortunately his speed was falling rapidly and only the engine and the first five coaches came into contact with the obstruction and no one was seriously injured.

Below: Class F. No 663 after the derailment at the foot of Ryhope Bank on 19 August 1889. / *Author's collection*

Right: Class F. No 663 at Gateshead awaiting entry to the Works. / *Author's collection*

Below right: Class M1. No 1622 (centre) after the Northallerton collision of 4 October 1894. The pilot engine, 2-4-0 No 905, is on the left with its tender on top! / *LPC*

Alex Davidson was one of the North Eastern drivers stationed at the NBR St Margarets shed in Edinburgh. In later years, when working from Haymarket shed, he had Z Atlantic 2193 before he took over Gresley Pacific 2564 *Knight of the Thistle.* He retired in 1935.

The Ulleskelf accident of 24 November 1906 did not, for once, concern an East Coast express, but this time it was a Scarborough-York-Leeds train which came to grief with Class F No 85 at its head. This was actually a Hull working and part of a triangular diagram Hull-Scarborough-Leeds-Hull of a type popular on the North Eastern before the introduction of the eight hour day in 1919.

By 1906 there were four tracks from York to Church Fenton and on occasions two trains running in the same direction appeared to be racing one another, although this was frowned on by the company. In this case the 7.05pm Lancashire & Yorkshire York to Manchester train was running on the up Normanton line, and a short distance behind was the train from Scarborough on the up Leeds line. However, ahead

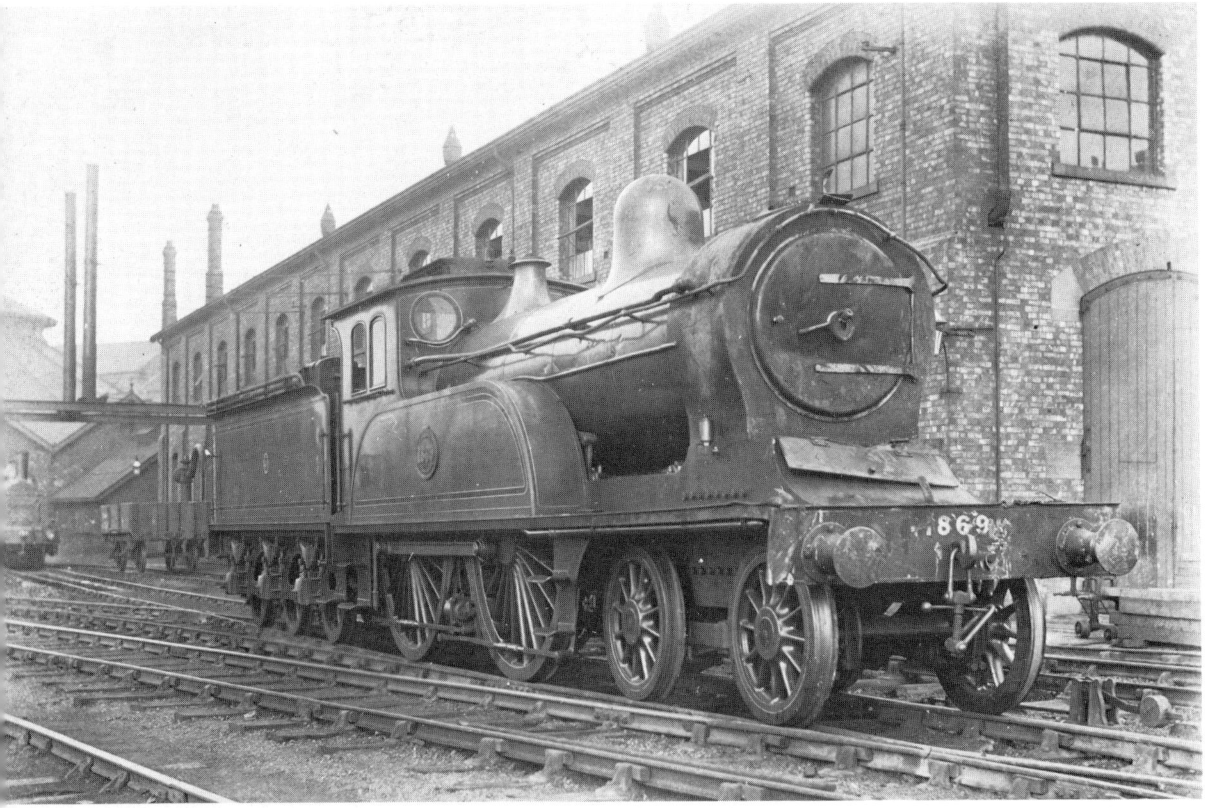
869

D
100254
EASTERN

Above left: Class Q1. No 1869 after the collision at Newcastle Central on 31 July 1897, when the fireman neglected to open one of the brake pipe cocks when coupling up at Berwick. */ Author's collection*

Left: Class F1. No 85 standing at York after the Ulleskelf collision of 24 November 1906, when a Scarborough-Leeds train ran into the rear of a stationary freight train. */ Author's collection*

Above: Class R. The heat of the sun buckled the rails at Felling on 26 March 1907 and 725, on a Liverpool-Newcastle express, was derailed. */ Author's collection*

there were two goods trains on the Leeds line and the signalmen had decided to divert the Leeds train on to the Normanton line at Bolton Percy so that it could overtake them. As the L&Y and the NER passenger trains were running almost together it was necessary to hold the North Eastern train at Bolton Percy until the L&Y train had cleared the section, before the Leeds train could be switched to the Normanton line to follow it. Consequently the Bolton Percy signalman kept his signals at danger, only to see the Leeds train pass them all at 50-60mph and continue into the section towards Ulleskelf, where it came into violent collision with the rear of the second goods.

The engine was very badly damaged and as the driver and fireman were killed it was never discovered why they had run past all the signals at danger. Fortunately passenger casualties were light and only seven were slightly injured. The engine was repaired and finished its days 26 years later — still working from Hull.

On 26 March 1907 another Liverpool-Newcastle train was derailed, this time the 8.35am from Liverpool, which left the rails at Felling, only 2½ miles from its destination. The train was worked by a Neville Hill Class R, No 725, with a Leeds crew.

The derailment was caused by the heat of the sun buckling the rails and this was actually seen from an overbridge by a deaf and dumb pedestrian. He pointed out the distorted rails to the driver of a steam roller passing over the bridge and the driver ran along the top of the cutting to Heworth signalbox, where he told the signalman what had happened. The Liverpool-Newcastle train was approaching the box but the signalman took no action and consequently the engine and all eight vehicles were derailed. Eight passengers were seriously injured and two subsequently died. The

Above: Class M1. A nasty derailment at Croft Spa on 14 June 1916, involving 1625. / *Author's collection*

Left and Above right: Class F1 and Class M1. In the disastrous head-on collision outside Hull Paragon on 14 February 1927, F1 No 96 on a train from Withernsea met M1 No 1628 on a train to Bridlington. Both engines were so badly damaged that they were considered not worth repairing and were scrapped. / *Author's collection*

engine fell over to the left against the south side of the cutting with the coaches — mainly LNWR — around it.

One of the 7ft 7¼in driving wheel engines, 1869, was involved in a second accident, this time at Middlesbrough on 1 January 1908 when working a New Year's Day excursion returning from Saltburn to Leeds. After passing signals at danger 1869 collided with the rear of a set of 18 four-wheel coaches being drawn into the station. Although the driver of 1869 estimated his speed at the time of the collision as 6 to 7mph the Inspecting Officer thought that it must have been much higher because of the extensive damage suffered by the engine, and the coaching stock of both trains. The two rear vehicles of the empty train were complete wrecks 'and one was reduced to matchwood'. Once again 1869 had its chimney knocked off.

On 5 April 1912 the tender of R1 No 1240 was derailed as it passed through connections at the north end of Eaglescliffe station when working the 4.05am mail train from York to Newcastle via Sunderland, which was running 68min late. In addition to the tender (which actually re-railed itself) all ten six-wheel vehicles forming the train were derailed but no one was injured. A small fire fed by gas from a broken pipe on one of the coaches was put out before it could get hold of the splintered woodwork.

The driver had never previously worked a train through Eaglescliffe without stopping and the

conclusion reached was that he had run through at an excessive speed. A speed limit of 15mph had been in force until the beginning of the year but since then it had been left to the discretion of the drivers to pass through at the speed they considered appropriate for safety.

It seems possible that the heavy R1 engines were more prone to derailment than the earlier — and lighter — classes of 4-4-0, for on 15 April 1918 No 1244 of the same class was derailed between Newby Wiske and Sinderby. Again the tender was thought to have been the first vehicle to be derailed, bringing off all nine vehicles forming the train. Again a small fire started below one of the derailed gas-lit coaches but it was extinguished before it gained a hold.

In the NER photograph files there are a number of views of an accident near Croft Spa on 14 June 1916, with both main line tracks blocked — one by a mineral train and the other by Class M No 1625 and its train of covered wagons, which had spread themselves liberally over the track. The cause of this accident is not known but it is believed to have been due to 1625 running into a derailed wagon (or wagons) of the mineral train. The photographs show that a military guard, complete with rifles, was put on the wreckage of 1625's train.

Two 4-4-0s were involved in the collision at Micklefield on 5 December 1915, again due to a driver passing signals at danger, this time during falling snow. The trains concerned were a York-Leeds and a Leeds-Hull; the former was derailed as it went over the junction, which was set for the Hull train, and although the driver of the latter braked when he saw a signal put to danger in front of him he was unable to stop before hitting the Leeds train across his path. The engines concerned were Class R No 1217 and Class M No 1622, the latter engine being one of the survivors of the Northallerton collision of 1894.

Two collisions with similar characteristics occurred at Selby, one in 1919 and one in 1921. In both cases a train leaving the platform was in collision with a train running through non-stop. On 8 August 1921 a relief express was running through on the up main, with GN 4-4-2 No 286 at the head, when it ran into a Bridlington-Leeds train which pulled out of the platform and on to the main line against the signals. The Leeds train was drawn by Class R No 2020.

As the McDonnell 4-4-0s were approaching extinction No 281 was derailed whilst running into York station on 1 June 1922. This was due to a grease knife being trapped between the left-hand switch rail and the stock rail. Due to the obsolete design of wedge type locking, still in use at the time, the signal could be pulled off even though the points were not fully home, leading to a derailment whilst running under clear signals! No 281 managed to survive until February 1923 and not only was it the last McDonnell 4-4-0 to run but it was the only McDonnell 4-4-0 to become LNER property at the Grouping of 1923.

For many years Selby had an allocation of McDonnell 4-4-0s, and one was outstationed at Low Moor (L&Y) for working the NER's York-Halifax and Hull-Halifax services. The driver at Low Moor — one John T. Healas — got into trouble a number of times whilst working McDonnell engines, and on one occasion he was rewarded for 'stopping very promptly and averting a collision at Ingham Siding, near Thornhill (L&Y) when working No 1498'. This was on 21 May 1904 and his promptness made him £1 better off! Four years later he received a strong caution for causing 1502 to be derailed at Low Moor. In March 1909 Healas was fined 7s 6d (37½p) for allowing his fireman to take charge of No 1502 on the 11.45am York-Selby and letting him run past the up platform starting signal at Selby. In the following year Healas himself passed a signal at danger in fog at Horbury Junction (L&Y) when working the 3.20pm Hull-Halifax. Later in 1910 he was in trouble for exceeding the speed limit over Naburn swing bridge with the 11.37am to Selby with engine 231.

Although trains had been hitting farm animals and farm carts on crossings for almost 100 years it was not until the twentieth century that the motorcar became a hazard on public and occupation crossings. The worst accident to happen in north eastern England occurred at Naworth (between Newcastle and Carlisle) on 30 August 1926, when an almost new 19-seat Halley char-a-banc was hit by Q No 1929 on the 1.18pm Newcastle to Carlisle express. Eight passengers in the char-a-banc and the gatekeeper were

killed. The accident was due to the incorrect operation of the gates by the porter in charge of the station.

The worst accident involving North Eastern 4-4-0s was the head-on collision outside Hull Paragon station on the morning of 14 February 1927. The two signalboxes controlling the exit from Paragon station were both electro-pneumatically operated and the accident was due, in part, to the efficient operation of the equipment. However, the main cause was the operation of a wrong lever by one of the signalmen in Park Street box anxious not to delay an incoming train from Withernsea carrying Hull businessmen, who soon complained if their train was late. As a train for Bridlington and Scarborough was leaving the station a signalman restored a signal immediately the engine had passed it and he then began setting the road for the incoming train. The wrong lever he pulled controlled facing points freed only after the signal had been restored and before the Scarborough train reached the locking bar of the points — an interval estimated at less than two seconds — and the result was that the departing train was diverted from an outgoing line to an incoming line on which the Withernsea train was running under clear signals.

The two trains met head-on near West Parade signalbox. Class D17/1 No 1628 was on the Scarborough train and Class D22 No 96 was on the train from Withernsea. The damage to both engines and their trains was extensive and both engines were considered to be beyond economical repair and were

Above left: Class G1. No 274 was run into by Atlantic 2205 at Darlington on 9 March 1929, and 274's tender was badly damaged. / *Author's collection*

Left: Class F1. No 777 was an unlucky engine. Here it is derailed at York after the driver ran past signals at danger on 1 November 1903. / *Author's collection*

Above: Class 3CC. This view of 1619, derailed when entering York station north end on 31 March 1920, also gives an idea of the North Eastern's liking for signals. Sixteen are visible! / *Author's collection*

subsequently scrapped. Unfortunately 12 passengers were killed and 24 suffered serious injury. No 96 was working from Botanic Gardens shed, and No 1628 from Bridlington shed on a Bridlington-Hull-Scarborough-Hull-Bridlington diagram.

Darlington was the site of two collisions in 1928/9, but although the worst (in 1928) did not involve a 4-4-0 the second, on 9 March 1929, caused severe damage to D23 No 274; in fact the tender of 274 was so badly damaged that it was replaced by the tender off D22 No 117, which had recently been withdrawn.

As with the previous collision at Darlington in April 1904 this accident was caused by a signalman forgetting a light engine standing on the main line, and by the driver not carrying out Rule 55 and informing the signalman of the vulnerable position of his engine. The light engine was run into by Atlantic 2205 on the 7.15pm mail from Newcastle to York.

During World War II North Eastern 4-4-0s were involved in at least two bombing incidents, both of which occurred in 1941. On 16 April D20 No 2108 was working the first train of the day from Pickering to York when it ran into a bomb crater near Coxwold, but it was not severely damaged in the soft earth and it was soon in traffic again. Then on 10 November D21 No 1242 was attacked by a German plane between Bempton and Speeton, where the Hull-Scarborough line runs near the east coast. A bomb was dropped but fortunately it did not explode as it passed right through the tender — in at the top and out at the back!

It is strange how some locations or engines are prone to mishaps of one sort or another. Over a spell of many years Goswick (on the East Coast main line south of Berwick) was the site of three derailments, all at the same set of facing points. In each case the engine overturned into the same ditch! From the above it will be seen that engine 1622 was involved in two collisions, and another unlucky engine was D20 No 1026, although fortunately not with serious results. On 27 September 1933 a connecting rod broke near Nafferton, but apart from damage to the splashers the result was not serious. Then three months later the same engine blew out a cylinder end on a Hull-Scarborough train just north of Bridlington. The one and only fitter stationed at the small shed at Bridlington had gone to the pictures with his wife and he had to be called by means of slides on the screens of the local cinemas to return and dismantle the engine! According to a local paper the mishap was due to 'the driving belt jamming' on 1026!

Another unlucky engine was Class F1 No 777, which was badly derailed at York on 1 November 1903. In LNER days it was notable as the black-sheep at Hull Botanic Gardens shed and this could explain why it was the engine chosen to go to Waskerley in July 1930 as a replacement for a withdrawn engine!

LNER Types

Top: Class D49. In 1927 Darlington Works built the first of a series of three-cylinder 4-4-0s to the designs of H. N. Gresley, the Chief Mechanical Engineer of the LNER from the company's formation in 1923. The first batch was fitted with piston valves operated by Gresley's 2:1 motion, and they were named after counties served by the LNER, the first being *Yorkshire*. Although not a North Eastern design they were a common sight in north eastern England, where most of their work was performed, although some did work in Scotland. / *British Rail*

Centre: Class D49. Later engines of the D49 class had rotary cam operated poppet valves and they were named after Hunts, with the nameplate surmounted by a brass replica of a running fox. The first of the 1932 engines was 201, *The Bramham Moor*. / *British Rail*

Above: Class D49. In 1942 No 365, *The Morpeth*, was rebuilt with two inside cylinders to the designs of Edward Thompson, making it the last of a long line of 4-4-0 engines built and operated in north eastern England. It was involved in a collision at Harrogate in November 1952, resulting in its premature withdrawal. / *British Rail*

17 Trains, Times and Trials

Speeds on the North Eastern in the last decade of the 19th century were not particularly fast. In 1893, when the Class M1 engines first appeared on the East Coast main line, the overall York to Edinburgh time for the 205 miles was 265min for the 10am from Kings Cross — the 'Scotch Express':

M	*Ch*			*pm*
00	00	YORK	dep	2.05
11	15	Alne	pass	2.20
22	16	Thirsk	pass	2.33
29	76	Northallerton	pass	2.42
44	10	Darlington	pass	2.58
56	77	Ferryhill	pass	3.14
66	07	Durham	pass	3.24
71	69	Chester-le-Street	pass	3.31
80	42	NEWCASTLE	arr	3.42
			dep	3.47
97	12	Morpeth	pass	4.09
115	31	Alnmouth	pass	4.30
132	14	Belford	pass	4.50
147	42	BERWICK	arr	5.08
			dep	5.13
158	63	Reston Junction	pass	5.29
175	63	Dunbar	pass	5.51
187	23	Drem	pass	6.05
205	04	EDINBURGH	arr	6.30

In the summer of 1900, when the first Class R engines were making a name for themselves, the timing was even easier; although the Newcastle stop has been extended by three minutes the five minute stop at Berwick had been abolished. This gave an average speed from York to Newcastle of 49.8mph, and from Newcastle to Edinburgh of 46.7mph.

When the well-known 75min booking between Leeds and Scarborough was introduced on 1 June 1900 the train was worked by the Worsdell 'singles' and it was not until the working was re-introduced in July 1922 (after being suspended during World War I) that the Class R engines appeared on this train. The train ran in the summer months only, mainly for the benefit of West Riding businessmen who were spending the summer on the coast with their families. Whilst the wife listened to the orchestra on the Spa and the 'nanny' looked after the children on the sands, the husband travelled to Leeds or Bradford to make more money, being whisked back to his family by this North Eastern 'flyer'. By 1922 the train was commencing its journey at Bradford (Forster Square) at 4.25pm and the Class R took over at Leeds (New Station) to work in the timing:

M	*Ch*			*pm*
00	00	LEEDS (New)	dep	4.58
4	33	Cross Gates	pass	5.04
9	56	Micklefield	pass	5.10
14	65	Church Fenton	pass	5.15
23	47	Chaloner Whin Junc.	pass	5.23
25	44	YORK	pass	5.26
32	12	Strensall	pass	5.35
46	56	Malton	pass	5.51
64	58	Seamer	pass	6.08
67	50	SCARBOROUGH	arr	6.13

The timing may not appear particularly fast — the average speed was 54mph — but when the slacks are taken into consideration it becomes apparent that some good work was required from the engine — and crew — if time was to be kept:

Location	*Speed*	*Remarks*
Micklefield	—	At driver's discretion over junction
Church Fenton	—	At driver's discretion over junction
York	15mph	Through station
Howsham Gates to Huttons Ambo	45mph	Curves for 4 miles
Malton	45mph	Through station
Seamer-Weaponness	45mph	Curves for ½ mile

Taking into account the long pull out of Leeds and the various slacks it is obvious that there was a need to gallop down the bank from Micklefield and then, after negotiating Church Fenton, to pick up speed again on the four-track section to York. By the time speed had been regained after passing through York the driver had only some seven miles before he had to start thinking of shutting off steam at Barton Hill in readiness for braking for the Kirkham Abbey curves, as the line twisted and turned to follow the River Derwent through the gap in the Howardian Hills. Once through Malton he had another 17 miles where he could run fast before slowing for Seamer. Speeds around 70mph appear to have been a regular occurrence, particularly down Micklefield Bank, and east of Malton, but the load was light — usually five non-corridor bogie coaches weighing about 130 tons. The Neville Hill Class R engine employed on this duty was from the allocation of seven — 725, 2011/3/20/6, 2108/9.

On 1 July 1902 an even faster working was introduced, but this time on the main line, when the 11.45am Newcastle to York was accelerated by two minutes between Darlington and York, making the allowance 43min for the 44 miles 10 chains. At first Class Q engines appear to have been responsible for this working although Class R engines made their appearance later. Fortunately R. J. Purves, the best photographer of North Eastern trains, used this train and a number of records have survived, by which time the train had been altered to leave Newcastle at 12.20pm and Darlington at 1.08. It was then due past Northallerton at 1.22, Thirsk 1.29½, Alne 1.40, and Poppleton Junction 1.48, with an arrival time at York of 1.51. The train then went on to Sheffield at 2.05 behind a Midland engine. The load from Newcastle to York was usually five non-corridor bogie vehicles.

The published records of runs behind various North Eastern 4-4-0s can usually be traced to a handful of enthusiastic recorders, such as Charles Rous-Marten who commenced writing the monthly series *British Locomotive Practice and Performance* in the September 1901 issue of the *Railway Magazine*. This series he continued to contribute until he died suddenly in April 1908 and he was followed by R. E. Charlewood from June 1908. In June 1909 a trio of contributors took over — W. J. Scott, J. F. Gairns, and C. J. Allen; C.J.A. actually became solely responsible for the series from the January 1911 issue (although in one of his books he claims it was from August 1909).

Logs of runs behind North Eastern engines were submitted by R. J. Purves and it was his timing of Class R No 1672 over the 44.1 miles from Darlington to York in 39min 34sec that first appeared in *The Railway Magazine* for October 1911. This log was repeated in the July 1913 issue and it subsequently appeared in Talbot's *Railway Wonders of the World*, published in fortnightly parts in 1913/14 and in other writings by C. J. Allen, as well as by O. S. Nock and others.

Another contributor of interesting runs was Charles Hylton Stewart, particularly when he was the organist at a church in Scarborough; he was a great friend of C. J. Allen and they often travelled together on the 6.05pm from York to Scarborough, which was booked to cover the 42 miles in 50min non-stop.

It is from these few men, therefore, that most of our knowledge comes concerning the day-to-day running on the NER. Full details can be obtained from the files of *The Railway Magazine* as there is not the space to reproduce them here; however, an index of runs is given in Appendix 7.

North Eastern engines ran to a number of unusual locations on special trains and, on a number of occasions ran through to London, usually on troop specials or excursions. For instance on 2 June 1900 Q No 1875, a Leeds engine, arrived at Kings Cross on a troop special, and six weeks later M1 No 1622 arrived at 'the Cross' on an excursion from Edinburgh, which it had presumably worked from York. On 2 July 1901 R No 2021 arrived at Kings Cross on five clerestory bogie coaches and returned light later the same day. The pioneer R, No 2011, was in London on 15 April 1905 on a troop special, as was Q No 1871: another R, No 2101 of York, arrived on 2 July 1905. On 13 and 15 January 1906 R No 2024 worked up on a train of 10 coaches to demonstrate the direct circulation system of steam heating, and to compare it with the storage system as used on a train of 15 GN six-wheel coaches. It was found that the NE train could be heated throughout in about 15min whereas the GN train took 75min.

Numerous trains were run to London in 1924 and 1925 for the British Empire Exhibition at Wembley and many of these were worked by North Eastern Area 4-4-0s, sometimes in pairs; classes noted comprised M, R and R1. Later, in the aftermath of the 1926 General Strike, some North Eastern 4-4-0s were drafted on loan to the Great Eastern section, these being Class F and Q engines.

As may be expected numerous trial runs with the 4-4-0s took place over the years, the earliest recorded being those between Saltburn, Darlington and Penrith in July, August and September 1885. On these tests nine-month-old McDonnell 4-4-0 No 126 was run for a week against a month-old Tennant 2-4-0 (1467) and a ten-year-old Fletcher 901 2-4-0 (156). No results appear to have been published, but for many years the passenger work on the line was handled by the 901 engines, and when they were withdrawn they were followed by the 'Tennants'. There is no trace of the

McDonnell engines working on the line and it can only be assumed that they were not too successful in the trials!

In 1896 Wilson Worsdell requested his Chief Draughtsman, Walter M. Smith, to carry out tests with various classes of engines between Newcastle and Tweedmouth using the London & North Western Railway's dynamometer car, which F. W. Webb had agreed to lend to the North Eastern. The car was in charge of C. E. Jones of Crewe and the North Eastern observers and assistants were R. J. Robson (draughtsman at Gateshead, who eventually became Chief Draughtsman in 1919); J. Weatherburn (also a draughtsman at Gateshead, who was appointed NER Dynamometer Car Inspector in 1912); and W. J. Smith.

The results of these trials were given in a paper presented by Walter M. Smith to the Institute of Mechanical Engineers in London on 27 October 1898; this paper was subsequently published as an excerpt from the Proceedings and it is well worth inspection even though lacking in a number of respects.

Among the mass of data one point that is not brought out is that the efficiency and reduced water consumption of the M1 4-4-0s had made non-stop running possible between Newcastle and Edinburgh in the Races to Aberdeen, which took place in 1895, the year before the dynamometer car trials. In the tests the two 2-4-0 engines left Newcastle with almost full tanks of water and it would appear that both had their tanks topped up before leaving. Even so the Fletcher 901 had only 567½ gallons remaining in the tank at Tweedmouth, and the Tennant had only 365 gallons. The J 'single' and the two 4-4-0s had tenders holding 3,940 gallons of water and each was some 700 gallons down when Newcastle was left: in this case, presumably, they were not topped up after leaving Gateshead shed. The consumption of each engine was:

	Locomotive		*Class*		
	901	1463	J	M1	Q1
Wheel arrangement	2-4-0	2-4-0	4-2-2	4-4-0	4-4-0
Tender capacity, gal	2,500	2,651	3,940	3,940	3,940
Water at Newcastle, gal	2,373	2,448	3,234	3,291	3,116
Water at Tweedmouth, gal	567.5	365	632	1,459	1,002
Water used, gal (for 65½ miles)	1,805.5	2,083	2,602	1,832	2,114
Water available for 59½ miles Tweedmouth to Edinburgh, gal	567.5	365	632	1,459	1,002

Consequently, with the load hauled on the trial trains not even the M1 engine could have run through non-stop from Newcastle to Edinburgh, but with just over half the load and, presumably, a full tank to start with, it was just possible with the 'racing' trains. The trial trains were allowed 75min for the 65½ miles to Tweedmouth, whereas Bob Nicholson and Tom Blades were through Berwick, 1½ miles beyond Tweedmouth and on the other side of the Royal Border Bridge, in exactly 60 minutes! Their hurry to get to Edinburgh before their water ran out must have been like the car driver caught speeding who, when asked why he was travelling so fast, said he was rushing home before he had an accident!

However, the installation of water troughs near Lucker in 1897 made regular non-stop running an everyday event, although marred initially by the dispute between the North Eastern and the North British regarding North Eastern engines working through from Berwick to Edinburgh.

18 Sheds and Duties

At Grouping Hull, and its sub-sheds at Bridlington and Doncaster, accounted for 46 of the 180 4-4-0s. The 11 D23s worked the local turns to Hornsea, Withernsea and Bridlington, with trips further afield if necessary, but the longer turns to Doncaster, York, Leeds and Scarborough were usually worked by the D17/1, D20 and D22 engines, the latter on the usually less important trains. The D20s were used on the heaviest trains, such as the 8.55am and 10.50am to Sheffield (Victoria); the 4pm to Liverpool (Lime Street); and the 5pm to Newcastle; which they worked as far as Leeds and York respectively.

Bridlington had a stud of seven D22s for working to Hull, Leeds, York and Scarborough, but in 1925 these were exchanged for eight D17/1 engines, giving Hull as many as 16 D22s. The Bridlington engines — 1622/8/9/30/4/5/8/9 — were joined by D19 No 1619 in 1926. Bridlington lost 1628 as a result of the Hull collision in February 1927 and this was the first of the class to go. Normal withdrawal commenced with 1635 in October 1931 and nine more engines were withdrawn from Bridlington over the years, the shed receiving in replacement first some D17/2 engines (1871/4/5, 1904/5/9/10), and later D20s 1078, 1234, 2016, 2024 and 2101.

Doncaster's three D17/1 engines were based at the former Great Northern shed for working to York and Hull, but this practice lasted only until 1925, when the workings were taken over by former Great Northern engines. Selby received two D17/1s (1631 and 1637) in 1925 for Hull, York, Leeds and Bridlington turns and they both remained there until withdrawn in 1934/5.

In the Northern Division Gateshead maintained a fleet of six D17/1s in 1923 for use mainly on the Carlisle line, but also on secondary workings on the main line to Darlington in the south and Alnmouth in the north. Main line workings to Newcastle were also covered by the one D17/1 at Alnmouth and the three at Tweedmouth; the latter were also called upon occasionally to work East Coast expresses when the top link engine was in trouble for steam, or had run hot. Tweedmouth lost its last D17/1 in March 1928 when 1624 and 1627 moved to Alnmouth to join 1621 and 1625, and Gateshead in March 1930 when 1632 and 1636 moved to Darlington. However, after a spell at Darlington and Northallerton 1636 returned north to Alnmouth and this two-road shed retained D17/1 engines until July 1945, when the famous 1621 was withdrawn for preservation.

Although 1621 managed to remain on passenger workings until 1945 the other of the class to survive World War II — 1629 — was not so fortunate. After becoming redundant at Bridlington in 1939 No 1629 was moved about from shed to shed — Hull, Leeds, Selby, Darlington, West Auckland, Middlesbrough and Newport; for a time in 1942 it was used by Middlesbrough for working down the coast to Scarborough, but when it reached Newport in 1943 it was used for banking freight trains up Picton bank on the Leeds Northern line to Northallerton.

In 1923 the 30 D17/2 engines were spread over only six sheds, with 5, 6, 7, and 8 at Neville Hill, Scarborough, West Hartlepool and Carlisle respectively. There were three at Gateshead and one (1922) at Starbeck. The Leeds and Scarborough engines both worked the important service linking the West Riding with the east coast and these trains provided important connections at York for passengers to and from Leeds: they also worked to Hull. The West Hartlepool engines worked mainly to Harrogate via Stockton, Eaglescliffe, Northallerton and Ripon, whilst the Carlisle engines, together with those at Gateshead, worked chiefly on the cross-country line which had started life in the 1830s as the Newcastle & Carlisle Railway. As a result of the Grouping the former North Eastern shed at Carlisle (London Road) was transferred to the Southern Scottish Area in 1925 and eventually the engines were concentrated at Canal shed — the former North British depot — where 1876 and 1921 remained until 1942: their last few months were spent in Edinburgh — 1876 working from Haymarket shed and 1921 from St Margarets. Another long established resident at Carlisle was 1901 but it was moved to Duns shed in April 1942 and returned to North Eastern Area stock in exchange for C15 4-4-2T No 9131.

From one D17/2 in 1923 Starbeck's allocation had increased to five in 1934 and Bradford, after an interval of ten years, received another D17/2 in 1935 in the shape of 1903; however, this was replaced by 1908 in August 1935 and 1925 in February 1938. When 1925 was withdrawn in November 1938 no replacement engine was provided as the LNER ceased to use the LMS shed at Manningham from 31 October 1938.

Scarborough lost 1903 to Starbeck in March 1933 when the NUR branch at Starbeck complained about the poor cab on D3 No 4313, and Scarborough's four remaining D17/2s departed in 1934 — 1878 to Darlington Works for scrapping, 1902 to Selby and 1906 and 1907 to West Hartlepool; the last two were displaced by new D49 engines.

Hull did not receive its first D17/2 until 1926 when 1909 and 1910 were moved south from Gateshead; in 1930 they were joined by 1922 from West Hartlepool, followed later by 1871, 1873, 1874, 1905, and 1907. Stockton had 1874 for a time in the 1930s and Alnmouth received its first example of the class in February 1933 when 1877 moved north from Leeds to replace D17/1 No 1636, due for scrapping according to official notes recording the transfer, but 1636 was not actually scrapped until five years later! Nos 1879 and 1906 followed to Alnmouth from West Hartlepool in April 1935, but a few months later 1879 was exchanged for 1923 of Starbeck as an engine with steam heating pipes at both ends was required for Alnmouth, leaving 1877, 1906 and 1923 to be withdrawn from Alnmouth in October and November 1938. However, Alnmouth saw D17/2 engines again in 1941 when Hull had no use for 1871 and 1873, and they were joined by 1905 from Selby in the following year. Although 1871 and 1905 were both withdrawn from Alnmouth, 1873 soldiered on and it eventually moved to York in July 1945, to join 1902.

At Leeds the two D18 engines, 1869 and 1870, took turns with the D17/2 engines on the workings to Scarborough and Hull until they were both withdrawn from service on the same day, 30 October 1930. No 1869's tender was subsequently used as a water carrier at Hulands Quarry, between Barnard Castle and Kirkby Stephen. Class D19 also became vacant in October 1930 with the scrapping of 1619, still a three-cylinder compound and still using saturated steam. In this case its tender was eventually transferred to D17/1 No 1905.

In 1923 the majority of the D20 engines were still at main line sheds, with 8 at Tweedmouth, 14 at Gateshead, 3 at Heaton, 7 at Darlington and 15 at York. Leeds had 7 and Hull 5, with the remaining one, 2012, at Blaydon. However, the main line sheds soon lost their D20s as they were displaced by larger and more modern engines, particularly in the 1930s, when sheds receiving D20s for the first time included Alnmouth (4), West Hartlepool (4), Stockton (1), Middlesbrough (2), Bridlington (2), and Haverton Hill (1). Starbeck received its first example in 1925 (2020) and twenty years later had an allocation of 15, working all but the very local services around Harrogate.

As a wartime measure Newport received six D20s in 1942/3 and these were used with 1629 (D17/1) on freight train banking duties, notably on Picton bank between Eaglescliffe and Northallerton. In 1923 the Tweedmouth engines were still working secondary trains on the main line — north to Edinburgh and south to Newcastle — but in 1947, at the end of the LNER, they were mainly employed on the Berwickshire branches to St Boswells, via Kelso or via Reston and Duns; in fact is was a D20 that worked the last train from Duns in September 1951.

As Alnmouth lost its D17/1s they were replaced by D17/2s which, in turn, were replaced by D20s. From four D20s in 1938 Alnmouth's allocation had grown to seven by 1948; as the class gradually disappeared to the scrapyard Alnmouth collected the stragglers until the last three — 62381 (1042), 62395 (1260) and 62396 (1665) — were withdrawn in November 1957, two on the 19th and 62395 on the 20th, making it the last survivor by one day! Attempts were made to have 62395 preserved by British Railways, but it was felt that sufficient North Eastern engines were already preserved and the sole concession was to have official photographs taken of the engine before it was scrapped; for this 62395 was given a fresh coat of black paint on one side only! It was cut up in February 1958, thus bringing to an end the long line of Worsdell 4-4-0s which had graced the East Coast main line for 70 glorious years!

During the 25 years existence of the LNER the ten D21 engines were distributed amongst only four sheds — originally York, Leeds and Starbeck — but York lost its engines in 1925 and Hull built up a small fleet of four for its Sheffield and York turns, the latter being the 5pm from Paragon, a restaurant car train for Newcastle. In 1931 all ten were shared between only two sheds, with eight at Neville Hill and two at Starbeck; the Leeds engines worked mainly to Scarborough, Hull and West Hartlepool, with occasional trips north to Newcastle at times of pressure. The Starbeck engines usually worked the Doncaster turns and the Pullman to Leeds. They were never popular engines, being considered too large for the work they performed.

After withdrawal in March 1943 No 1241 was fitted

with a 48-year-old tender (off J24 No 1846) and sent to South Wales for Royal Air Force target practice: it was despatched from Darlington on 24 March 1943 bound for Fishguard via Banbury. The remains were eventually returned to Darlington for scrapping.

The D22 engines were, in LNER days, mainly stationed in the Southern Division, with 31 divided between Hull, Bridlington, Selby, Scarborough and Starbeck, and the remaining six between Alnmouth (1), Gateshead (1), Waskerley (1) and Carlisle (3). The Alnmouth engine (No 18) worked on the Alnwick and Coldstream branch, on the Amble branch, and on the main line north and south to Berwick and Newcastle respectively. The Gateshead engine (1546) worked to Darlington and across to Carlisle, whilst the Waskerley engine (663) made two return trips a day between Blackhill and Darlington. The Carlisle engines appear to have worked on carriage shunting duties between Citadel station and the North Eastern Area yard at London Road, and on passenger duties on the Newcastle line as far as Haltwhistle. All three at Carlisle — 154, 355 and 1324 — were withdrawn in the first two months of 1930.

Botanic Gardens shed at Hull had eleven D22s in 1923, with a further seven at Bridlington, all working trains in an area bounded by Doncaster-Selby-Leeds-York-Scarborough-Withernsea. Thus they were a very common sight on trains of North Eastern coaches, usually on semi-fasts and slow trains, although they did occasionally appear on expresses. For a short period two D22s (808 and 1538) were stationed at Springhead — the former Hull & Barnsley Railway shed at Hull — to help out the five Hull & Barnsley Kitson-built 4-4-0s, and the rapidly disappearing Beyer Peacock 2-4-0s which dated from the opening of the line in 1885.

From Springhead 1538 went to Scarborough, working to Hull and York, whilst 808 eventually finished up at Stockton until it was scrapped in 1930. For a few months in 1926 it was shedded at Malton for use as station pilot, where it replaced a McDonnell 0-6-0 which had been withdrawn. Selby had five D22s which worked to Hull, Leeds and Bridlington and one, 1537, remained at Selby until it was withdrawn in November 1935: it was the last of the class to remain in use.

When Bridlington's allocation of D22s was exchanged for D17/1s in 1925 Hull's fleet of the former rose to 16 and remained at this total until No 96 was involved in the Hull collision in February 1927. No 663 from Gateshead in exchange for D20 No 2110 brought the total up to 16 again in January 1929. In February 1929 withdrawal began in earnest and 514 went for scrap, followed in March by 117; at the same time the last of the class in the north, 1546, moved down from Tweedmouth. Over the next six years — 1929 to 1935 — 16 D22s were withdrawn from Hull, the last being 1546 in January 1935. In the same period two D22s were moved away from Hull — 777 to Waskerley in July 1930 to take up the Blackhill-Darlington working, and 115 to Starbeck in April 1931 to join 1533 and 1545, both withdrawn later the same year. In October 1931 No 115 moved to Bradford (to replace D23 No 328) and was itself withdrawn in December 1933, still working from Manningham shed.

The D23s, the smallest of the Worsdell 4-4-0s, were in 1923 still based mainly in the south of the former NER system, with 11 at Hull, three at Scarborough, three at Starbeck, one at Malton and one at Bradford; the most northerly was 372 at Darlington. Over the next few years the position changed and Scarborough and Hull lost their allocation: some moved north to Tweedmouth and the sub-shed at Duns (223 and 258) but 23, after a short spell at Tweedmouth, settled down at Waskerley. However, it was in the Darlington area where the most notable changes took place, as 15 were divided between Darlington (8), Barnard Castle (3), Middleton-in-Teesdale (1) and Kirkby Stephen (3), to work the line over Stainmore Summit to Tebay and Penrith, replacing Fletcher and Tennant 2-4-0s.

Withdrawal commenced in August 1929 with No 23 from Waskerley; nine more went to the scrapheap in 1930, five in 1931 and four in 1933, leaving the sole survivor, 1120, to be withdrawn from Bradford in May 1935.

Appendices

1 ALLOCATION OF NER 4-4-0s IN 1907

	F1	G1	M	M1	Q	Q1	R	38	
Blaydon	-	-	-	1	-	-	-	1	
Carlisle	3	-	-	-	-	-	-	1	
Darlington	-	-	-	2	-	-	-	2	
Edinburgh	-	-	-	-	-	-	2	-	
Gateshead	6	-	-	3	13	-	26	1	
Heaton	-	-	-	-	4	-	2	-	
Hull	8	16	1	2	-	-	-	2	
Leeds	15	-	-	-	4	2	8	1	
Scarborough	4	-	-	-	-	-	-	2	
Starbeck	-	3	-	-	-	-	-	1	
Tweedmouth	-	-	-	7	1	-	8	-	
York	1	1	-	5	8	-	14	1	
Selby	-	-	-	-	-	-	-	16	
Total	37	20	1	20	30	2	60	28	Total 198

2 ALLOCATION OF NER 4-4-0s IN 1923

	F	G	M	Q	Q1	R	R1	3CC	
Alnmouth	1	-	1	-	-	-	-	-	
Blaydon	-	-	-	-	-	1	-	-	
Bradford (Manningham)	-	1	-	-	-	-	-	-	
Bridlington	7	-	-	-	-	-	-	-	
Carlisle	3	-	-	8	-	-	-	-	
Darlington	-	1	-	-	-	7	-	-	
Doncaster (GN)	-		3	-	-	-	-	-	
Gateshead	1	-	6	3	-	14	-	-	
Heaton	-	-	-	-	-	3	-	-	
Hull	13	11	7	-	-	5	-	1	
Leeds	-	-	-	5	2	7	2	-	
Malton	-	1	-	-	-	-	-	-	
Scarborough	4	3	-	6	-		-	-	
Selby	5	-	-	-	-	-	-	-	
Starbeck	2	3	-	1	-	-	1	-	
Tweedmouth	-	-	3	-	-	8	-	-	
Waskerley	1	-	-	-	-	-	-	-	
West Hartlepool	-	-	-	7	-	-	-	-	
York	-	-	-	-	-	15	7	-	
Total	37	20	20	30	2	60	10	1	Total 180

3 ALLOCATION OF NER 4-4-0s IN 1947

	D17/2	D20	
Alnmouth	-	7	
Bridlington	-	4	
Duns	-	1	
Hull	-	6	
Northallerton	-	3	
Selby	-	9	
Starbeck	-	15	
Tweedmouth	-	3	
West Hartlepool	-	5	
York	2	-	
Total	2	53	Total 55

4 LOCOMOTIVE REQUISITIONS AND ORDER NUMBERS (FROM 1891)

Reqn No	*Date*	*Order No*	*Quantity*	*Class*	*Works*	*Completed*	*Engine Nos*
6	18-2-92	——	20	F1	Gateshead	Cancelled	—
7	21-4-92	——	1	M	Gateshead	5/93	1619
		L381	20	M1	Gateshead	2/94	1620-39
20	31-10-95	L103	2	Q1	Gateshead	6/96	1869/70
		L101	10	Q	Gateshead	12/96	1871-80
24	23-7-96	A111	10	Q	Gateshead	6/97	1901-10
		A113	10	Q	Gateshead	11/97	1921-30
31	15-9-98	A121	10	R	Gateshead	12/99	2011-20
34	19-10-99	A123	10	R	Gateshead	12/00	2021-30
		A133	10	R	Gateshead	5/01	2101-10
50	22-6-05	A25	10	R	Gateshead	12/06	476, 592, 707, 708, 711/2/3, 723/4/5
51	14-6-06	A31	10	R	Gateshead	6/07	1026/42, 1147, 1206/9/17/32/4/6/60
		A33	10	R	Gateshead	10/07	1051/78, 1184, 1207/10/23/35/58, 1665/72
63	9-1-08	381	10	R1	Darlington	8/09	1237-46

6 MILEAGES BETWEEN GENERAL REPAIRS

Class of engine	*NER May 1917*	*LNER Feb 1932*
F/D22	60,000	60,000
G/D23	60,000	50,000
M/D17/1	75,000	70,000
Q/D17/2	75,000	70,000
Q1/D18	75,000	70,000
R/D20	85,000	70,000
R1/D21	85,000	70,000
3CC/D19	50,000	—
38/—	50,000	—

5 NER 4-4-0 CYLINDERS, VALVE GEAR AND WHEELS

	D 1324	D 340	F	F1	F1 Reb	G1 2-4-0	G1 4-4-0	M
Cyl Dia HP	18in	18in	18in	18in	18in	17in	18in	20in
Cyl Dia LP	26in	26in	26in	—	—	—	—	28in
Cyl Stroke	24in	24in	24in	24in	24in	24in	24in	26in
Valves—Slide/ Piston	SV	PV	SV	SV	PV	SV	PV	SV
Valves—Above Below	A	A	A	A	B	A	B	Outside
Valve gear; Joy/ Stephenson	J	J	J	J	S	J	S	S
Frames; length	25ft 11in	?	28ft 1in	28ft 1in	28ft 1in	?	27ft 1½in	30ft 5in
Driving Wheels	6ft 8¼in	6ft 8¼in	6ft 8¼in	6ft 8¼in	6ft 8¼in	6ft 1¼in	6ft 1¼in	7ft 1¼in
Leading/Bogie wheels	4ft 7¼in	4ft 7¼in	3ft 7¼in	3ft 7¼in	3ft 7¼in	4ft 1¼in	3ft 1¼in	3ft 7¼in

	3CC	M1 *	M1 Reb	Q	Q Reb **	Q1	Q1 Reb ***	R +	R1
Cyl Dia HP	19in	19in	19in	19½in	19in/ 19½in	20in	19in/ 20in	19in	19in
Cyl Dia LP	20in	—	—	—	—	—	—	—	—
Cyl Stroke	26in HP 24in LP	26in	26in	26in	26in	26in	26in	26in	26in
Valves—Slide/ Piston	PV-HP SV-LP	SV	PV	SV	PV	SV	PV	PV	PV
Valves—Above Below	B-HP Outside-LP	Outside	A	A	A	A	A	B	A
Valve gear; Joy/ Stephenson	S	S	S	S	S	S	S	S	S
Frames; length	30ft 5in	30ft 5in	30ft 5in	30ft 5in	30ft 5in	30ft 11in	30ft 11in	30ft 11in	33ft 0in
Driving Wheels	7ft 1¼in	7ft 1¼in	7ft 1¼in	7ft 1¼in	7ft 1¼in	7ft 7¼in	7ft 7¼in	6ft 10in	6ft 10in
Leading/Bogie wheels	3ft 7¼in	3ft 7¼in	3ft 7¼in	3ft 7¼in	3ft 7¼in	3ft 7¼in	3ft 7¼in	4ft 0in	3ft 7¼in

Notes * One engine with piston valves
** 19in dia cylinders fitted from February 1914
*** 19in dia cylinders fitted to 1869 March 1920
+ Length of Raven frames 31ft 1⅛in

7 INDEX OF RUNS RECORDED IN THE RAILWAY MAGAZINE

Vol	*Page*	*Class of engine*	*Location*
IX	270	R	Darlington-York
XVI	18	Q	Darlington-York
XXVI	148	R & R1	Darlington-York
XXVI	284	R1	York-Newcastle and Newcastle-Edinburgh
XXVIII	367	R1	Darlington-York
XXIX	305	R	Darlington-York
XXX	496	R & R1	York-Darlington
XXXI	396	R	Newcastle-Edinburgh and Edinburgh-Newcastle
XXXII	198	R1	Darlington-York
XXXIII	38	M & R	Darlington-York
XXXV	22	R & R1	York-Newcastle
XXXV	208	G, R & R1	Bridlington-York Hull-Filey and York-Scarborough
XXXVI	44	R	Harrogate-Darlington
XXXVII	115	R	Darlington-York

8 MILEAGES

Class D17/1

No	*Mileage*	*No*	*Mileage*	*No*	*Mileage*
1620	1,213,737	1627	977,629	1633	1,210,269
1621	1,499,944*	1628	?	1634	995,018
1622	1,367,604	1629	1,358,002*	1635	1,056,727
1623	1,066,850	1630	1,183,102	1636	1,153,421
1624	1,179,915	1631	1,172,100	1637	984,312
1625	1,044,483	1632	1,057,072	1638	1,302,820
1626	1,261,417			1639	1,150,531

* mileage at 31 December 1942. These two engines continued to run until 1945

Class D17/2

No	*Mileage*	*No*	*Mileage*	*No*	*Mileage*
1871	?	1901	?	1921	?
1872	1,151,786	1902	1,276,208	1922	1,020,961
1873	1,478,596	1903	1,120,312	1923	1,313,820
1874	1,206,245	1904	1,201,262	1924	1,169,912
1875	1,111,131	1905	?	1925	1,204,200
1876	?	1906	1,246,608	1926	1,039,879
1877	1,351,238	1907	993,601	1927	1,048,496
1878	1,110,402	1908	1,248,042	1928	1,094,587
1879	?	1909	1,187,212	1929	1,132,394
1880	1,081,615	1910	1,232,792	1930	987,305

Class D18

No	*Mileage*	*No*	*Mileage*
1869	1,062,695	1870	1,089,057

Class D19

No	*Mileage*
1619	909,331

Class D20

No	*Mileage*	*No*	*Mileage*	*No*	*Mileage*
476	1,253,975	2011	2,017,586	2028	1,494,071
708	1,110,512	2012	1,534,377	2102	1,582,419
713	1,274,448	2013	1,682,622	2103	1,683,979
725	1,145,240	2015	1,424,503	2104	1,436,088
1051	1,397,479	2019	1,541,019	2105	1,593,629
1223	1,307,558	2021	1,424,319	2106	1,458,437
1232	1,247,319	2024	1,495,845	2107	1,536,334
1236	1,263,046	2025	1,445,144	2108	1,522,479
		2027	1,488,642	2110	1,540,175

Class D22

No	*Mileage*	*No*	*Mileage*	*No*	*Mileage*
18	1,120,537	356	1,114,649	1532	1,163,987
42	1,124,565	514	1,168,879	1533	1,298,408
85	1,338,892	663	1,175,997	1534	1,267,983
96	?	673	1,276,964	1535	1,253,205
115	1,244,491	684	1,173,234	1536	1,289,954
117	1,101,720	777	1,522,701	1537	1,344,425
154	1,262,245	779	1,041,013	1538	1,056,647
194	1,325,826	803	1,167,765	1539	1,270,146
230	1,290,361	808	1,254,166	1540	1,229,514
340	1,366,250	1137	1,330,267	1541	1,347,219
355	1,052,170	1324	1,315,590	1542	1,195,167
				1543	1,129,238
				1544	1,000,085
				1545	1,223,360
				1546	1,221,616

Class D23

No	*Mileage*	*No*	*Mileage*	*No*	*Mileage*
23	1,246,931	328	1,143,597	675	1,286,795
214	1,608,844	337	1,240,328	676	1,260,823
217	1,340,642	372	1,330,112	677	1,354,605
222	1,120,749	472	1,167,300	678	1,261,050
223	1,358,741	521	1,131,184	679	1,284,722
258	1,280,023	557	1,259,123	1107	1,235,744
274	1,119,424			1120	1,205,618